PARASITES INSIDE ME

The Enemies Within

By Karrie Sicely

Directed By Lisa Honeywell

ISBN-9798469707165
ISBN-10: 1477123456

Cover design by: Lisa Honeywell
Library of Congress Control Number: 2018675309
Printed in the United States of America

MEDICAL DISCLAIMER

◆ ◆ ◆

Parasites Inside Me author Karrie Sicely makes no promises, guarantees, representations and or warranties regarding medical diagnosis and or medical treatment, and is neither diagnosing, preventing, nor treating specific health challenges.

You are solely responsible for your own medical care. All opinions and statements in this book are mine. They are not that of my endorsements.

Karrie Sicely

◆ ◆ ◆

CONTENTS

FOREWORD

◆ ◆ ◆

Robin M. Overstreet, Ph.d.

Professor Emeritus – Division Of Coastal Sciences, Marine Parasitology And Pathobiology

Karrie's desire to find answers brought us together where we became friends. Her desire to learn about parasites and her drive to find resolve to her medical problems related to parasites shows her determination. I was happy to help her learn and assist her in getting the help she needed.

◆ ◆ ◆

ENDORSEMENTS

Dr. Eldon Beard

Karrie's relentless determination insured her family was always properly cared for. Upon learning of her own medical issues, by the grace of God and her trust in me led her to find the help to get her life back.

◆ ◆ ◆

Dr. Jordan Axe; Axe Holistic Medicine

Karrie's research with my knowledge assisted me in addressing her lingering medical issues. Her suffering was eliminated using both traditional and holistic care. The treatment modalities noted in her book may be a valuable resource to anyone suffering

Judy A. Mikovits, Phd

NYT Best Selling Author, Plague of Corruption

Karrie details her incredible journey in a system desperate for more research into the role of parasitic infection in chronic disease. A must read.

◆ ◆ ◆

William Panzarella, Author

In her eloquent and well-researched book, Parasites Inside Me, Karrie Sicely delves into not just a personal topic, but an extremely important and sadly much underreported one. Though thorough it is written in a way that anyone can follow and understand and more importantly to learn. It is a must read.

PREFACE

◆ ◆ ◆

There are millions of living things in the world that are astonishing, yet mysteriously strange parasites are never a thought or consideration.

They are all around us and in every patch of dirt. They are transmitted in many ways to include vectors like mosquitoes and snails and yet we have little surveillance of them.

Parasites can enter your food, water, and your community pools. They can be transmitted by your animals and even you! You cannot see them when they attack, but soon the effects may cripple your mind and body.

Parasites are not something we discuss in this country, but they are very real. It is not something you will hear on the evening news, read in the newspaper, or even watch in a thriller movie.

This is my story of dealing with the enemies from within. The shame, embarrassment, and pain to everyone involved has become the hidden secret people do not talk publicly about. Due to the disbelief that parasites invade the human body, medical support and for some, even family support proves to be challenging for many.

In the United States and around the world, individuals suffering with parasites are desperately seeking help to be free of these destructive creatures. Millions searching for anyone who can or will help, only to find none. They dream of the life they once knew and loved, now gone.

The battle to get into Infectious Disease doctors for many, is anything but possible causing many to give up. These people are spending thousands of dollars and every penny they have seeking help. Numerous people have even taken their own lives from the lack of treatment and respect, from those with the ability to help.

The label of "Delusional Parasitosis" from many doctors is all too common for those who suffer with parasites in their stools and body. It is interesting how 130 million Americans could be so delusional all while showing many medical issues caused by parasites. While I was not one to receive this diagnosis, there are many who do. I would not have accepted a demeaning and false diagnosis.

The opinions in this book are mine based off the research and experiences that I have had. They do not represent that of any of my endorsements or any affiliations of any other person.

◆ ◆ ◆

This book is dedicated to every individual battling a parasitic infection.

This is my story, the opinions in this book are mine, and solely mine. I am not encouraging the use of products that I have utilized in my treatment.

Names of some of the doctors have been changed, however my story is true and accurate.

ACKNOWLEDGEMENTS

◆ ◆ ◆

Dr. Robin Overstreet: God led me to Dr. Overstreet who was instrumental in sharing his wealth of knowledge as well as utilizing my microscope pictures to identify cysticercosis as one of my parasites.

Dr. Beard: My family doctor who took phenomenal care of my family. It is only by God's grace and Dr. Beard's compassion that I am alive.

Dr. Expert: From my first visit with Dr. V and his staff were wonderful. His utilization of my pictures allowed him to identify that I had tapeworms and round worms.

Dr. Axe: God's guidance and direction led me to Dr. Axe who was instrumental in resolving the massive pain I had related to my irritable bowel syndrome. His continued care has been immeasurable in helping me to remove my remaining parasites.

Dr. W: She was an enormous emotional support, Dr. W was the only physician who was able to get to the root cause of my UTI, urinary tract infections. Her continued compassion and empathy have had a profound impact on my ability to get back to healthy living.

Lori Kisner – RN: My sister Lori invested much of her time

researching as well as being a huge emotional support for me in this journey.

Brent Sicely: My husband was initially challenged to understand my condition later becoming my champion researcher and support system.

Kisha Thompson: My daughter made me laugh when I stopped laughing; she worked to bring laughter back into my life.

Katrina Speight: A believer from the beginning. My daughter was supportive, taking me for medical procedures, sending me flowers and balloons to uplift my spirits and still does.

Brent Sicely Jr.: My son went beyond doing things to lighten my load around the house, his tenderheartedness is much appreciated.

Derrick Earley: My prior co-worker restored my faith, constantly praying over me at a time when my faith was broken.

Jackie Spisak: My neighbor was a skeptic initially, upon witnessing one of my worms became a believer and remained supportive of me through this medical maze.

Charity Lee Armistead-Carroll: She is a fellow sufferer in Texas who has done much research related to parasitic infections. We collaborate on many different studies to understand the pathology of parasites.

Tina Palisi did an amazing job of editing my Ps and Qs. Although she recommended that I refrain from using language that may be offensive, I had to go with my gut. I said exactly what I truly feel.

Dr. Leslie Pierce: Dr. Leslie was led to me by her daughter who was searching for information related to parasitic infections.

This connection led me to my publisher, Lisa Honeywell.

Lisa Honeywell: This book would not have been possible without Lisa's guidance. Her magical ways with words and vast knowledge of how and when to do everything related to publishing a book all came together for me.

CHAPTER 1: THE BEGINNING

Well Water

We had been living in a 3-story townhouse in Northern VA for about 6 months when our landlord decided to sell the home. This left us little time to find a place to live. We started searching for vacant homes and found two that would accommodate our budget.

I had scheduled appointments to see the homes to determine if either were what we were looking for. The first house we saw was small and in a rundown area, and the other in a country setting.

We chose the house that was placed in the country and moved in June 2013. This home was on a well water system that we were initially happy about. It was one less bill to have. We had little knowledge about well water systems, and we were not aware of the dangers that they could pose. The home also had a water softener system, that we assumed, wrongfully, would clean the water.

For the 3.5 years of our tenancy, there had never been an inspection on the well nor was the water tested. This was of no concern to us at the time because we didn't know this should be done yearly.

Standard testing recommendations are at intervals of every spring for mechanical and every year (according to the CDC) for nitrates, coliform, fecal coliform, volatile organic compounds, and pH. It was not a thought to me at the time.

Later when we moved out, in December of 2016, we learned that the property owner of the home we rented from was diagnosed with cancer. This is an important topic to remember as I tell my story and divulge the research.

My story began in 2014, when I suddenly had severe pain in one of my toes on my right foot. I had not hit my toe on anything and was clueless at to what could have triggered it. As I checked my toe, I noticed that I had a small pinhole at the end of it and was intrigued how this could have happened. We had lived in this home for about a year at this time.

Please visit: TheParasiteLady.com to see related images.

The injured toe just happened to be my long toe next to my big toe. It had crossed my mind that a dog hair had penetrated my skin, so I removed my shoes and soaked my foot in Epsom salt to help alleviate the pain. At that point, I decided that I needed to try to remove whatever had penetrated my skin. I grabbed a sewing needle and clippers and sterilized them. I began to dig into the hole and dug until the pain was too much to bear, but I saw nothing at that point.

I began to reflect on any incidents I may have had that would have caused this. Occasionally I did walk in the grass barefoot as I had many times in my life but didn't recall a time of stumbling or injuring it. The hole in my toe would continue to cause pain and would remain until January 5, 2020.

Granuloma Growth

Only months after the pinhole in my toe on my right foot, I acquired a mole on the back of my right ankle about the size of a dime. This mole was different than the other moles I had in color and shape. It was round and would sometimes protrude from my skin and sometimes it would be flat but was ever changing. It was painful and had an achy feeling when it was protruding, which is the only reason I even noticed it.

Because skin cancer was in my family medical history, I became concerned, and began to look for a dermatologist nearby. I found only one within an hour of our home and called to schedule an appointment.

Traditionally doctors always ask about family history related to cancer, because the thought is that it can be transmitted genetically. As I take you through my journey, I want you to remember that thought of transmission.

A few days later, I arrived for my appointment with my husband and son in tow. We were the only patients in the lobby, so the wait to be taken to the exam room was brief.

After the nurse checked my vitals, the doctor arrived to hear my concerns about the mole. He began his observations and said "Ah yes, I have seen these before, these moles have roots. I can remove it, but the chances of it growing back are pretty high."

I had never heard this before, not that I had much involvement with the medical field, but it made little sense to me at all. His words did not sit right with my soul. I wasn't really concerned if it would grow back, I just wanted it removed and tested for cancer.

As I looked away the doctor went on to numb the area of the mole, cut it out and send it off to the lab for testing. Not long after the results came back negative for cancer.

This was good news, and I was happy with the results, but it still didn't answer how this thing just suddenly appeared from thin air. As it turned out the doctor was wrong, the mole never did grow back!

Veins Blocked

During this time of sudden moles and a hole in my toe, I developed what looked like fat rolls on my legs just above my knees. I was not over-weight at the time.

These areas became achy causing me to use a heating pad and massaging the pain. This only relieved the discomfort for a brief time, so I decided to try some Aspercreme gel for the muscle pain.

The pain continued to increase, and my legs began to feel heavy as time progressed. While it was not debilitating, both the look and the achy feelings were annoying. I began to consume Ibuprofen daily for the discomfort, but it brought little relief.

It was only after I started to research the symptoms that I found that it could be caused from blocked arteries in my legs. There were several articles that popped up that led me to Dr. Leg, who I called to make an appointment.

On the scheduled day, I arrived and checked in and was taken back to the exam room. While visiting with the doctor, I explained what was happening while showing him my legs. I asked if blocked arteries could be the cause and he felt like it could be but wanted to have an ultrasound to confirm. The doctor then sent me to the clerk to schedule this procedure.

It was just a simple ultrasound on the legs and was nothing invasive or painful. Upon arriving to have this procedure done, I was taken back to the exam room where I got up on the bed. As the technician explained the process, she positioned the monitor in a way that allowed me to observe the images. She was not permitted to answer any questions of findings.

It only took a day or so to get the results, showing that I had blockages in the secondary veins. The doctor believed this could be the reason for the heavy feeling in my legs as well as the pain and fatty deposits. He wasn't overly concerned about this being detrimental to my health so neither was I. The office had scheduled me for a procedure to cauterize those veins that would force the body to re-route the blood.

Both of my legs were scheduled to be done on the same day at the doctor's office which was connected to the hospital. This was comforting to be so close in case anything went wrong.

The day of the procedure came, and I entered the facility with my pre-purchased stockings in hand. Having some feelings of being nervous, I was taken back to the procedure room and given a gown to change into. It was very much like an operating room in a hospital just on a much smaller scale.

It was disturbing for me to be awake through the process of the cauterizations and hearing the difficulties they had. The doctor had a small issue getting the needle through one of the blockages in my leg which caused me to worry a little.

I worked hard to distract my thoughts instead of focusing on what they were saying. The procedure took about an hour but felt like an eternity. After the procedure was competed, they put my compression stockings on me, and I was free to leave. I left the facility and headed to work.

A couple of weeks later, I had my follow-up appointment where I was told that my issues were now resolved, and my symptoms should be alleviated.

As I was waiting to see the changes, more issues had arisen. The symptoms had expanded to impact my hips, right ankle, right shoulder, and feet. I wondered if it was my shoes causing these issues, or maybe it was the bulging discs in my back, or even the miles, I walked each day at work. I didn't know but I was entertaining every possible cause.

My hips felt as though I had run for many miles. The pain would shoot down my left leg and had been intermittent for a long time. I had wondered if my bulging discs were pinching my sciatica nerve. My right ankle ached tremendously, and my right shoulder felt like it was overworked and exhausted. My vision started to decline requiring me to get readers to see my work on the computer. It appeared I was falling apart quickly.

I had gone back to see the doctor and explained that the pain had traveled to different areas. The Doctor scheduled another ultrasound on my new areas of concern showing more veins were being blocked. After discussing the results of the second ultrasound with the doctor, he was going to perform the same procedure on these newly blocked veins. Going through this a second time was not something I was looking forward to.

One of the most important aspects of my job was interacting with customers. We always talked to our customers including topics not related to their visits. The engagements made our customers feel important and allowed us to build relationships with them. Utilizing these skill sets, we beat our sales target by

2.3 million for the year.

This one particular day, I had a frequent customer who entered, and we began to talk as we usually did. After assisting him with his product needs, I listened to his stories and he to mine.

I began to tell him about the surgery that I had done a few weeks prior and spoke of the upcoming procedure. His advice changed my way of thinking; "don't do it, you can never get those veins back and they will just keep taking and taking."   His words would have real meaning in just a few more years.

I hadn't had many interactions with the medical field up to this point, but what the customer said, made me think. He was a much older gentleman and because of that I was more attentive to his advice. I heeded his words and opted not to do this second procedure. Instead, I worked to change my diet as best I could. I cancelled my procedure and wouldn't see another doctor for a couple of years.

I was never a healthy eater and ate many carbs and junk foods throughout my life. I didn't eat a lot of meat or fresh vegetables. My choice of food was pizza, pasta, chips, and pop. It was time to re-focus my energy to improve my diet.

My husband and I discussed the dietary changes that we would immediately make in our food selections. Instead of store-bought meat, we would find a local butcher who provided meats raised without antibiotics and hormones. It was important to ensure the meats we purchased were American raised that were grass-fed and had no injections of chemicals.

The repeal of the Cool Act of 2015 allows meats to be imported and repackaged in the US and to have a "Product of USA" label on them.

The World Trade Organization (WTO) sued the US on behalf of Canada, Mexico, and Brazil because Americans did not want to purchase their meats.

A no name republican drafted the repeal of the COOL Act, which is only misleading the American people, because there is no way to decipher where the meat really came from.

Statistics show that about 75% of the meats in grocery stores are imported. This misleading bill has a massive impact on the health of Americans. From February 2017 to February 2020 beef from Brazil was paused due to the confirmation of criminal behaviors of the meat inspectors.

Many are not aware that this part of the Tariff act of 1930 was repealed. Many other countries had banned the meat from Brazil long before the US did, and still have their ban in place.

I found an article on pbs.org called "Modern Meat," Dr. Glenn Morris who has done studies about this topic suggested that the sub-therapeutic antibiotic use in these animals is likely to cause health issues for humans.

The tetracycline given to the animals adds about 3% weight, allowing for bigger profit margins. These antibiotics make animals bigger faster.

These medicines are possibly causing drug resistance in humans. The US has not banned the administration of these antibiotic treatments in the animals we consume like the EU and Canada have.

Electromagnetic Energy

I t wasn't long before I started to notice that I could hear what I thought to be electromagnetic waves in my house.

Every day I would hear these humming sounds very loudly. The pitch would change to be high or low and the intensity would increase or decrease. I had asked my husband if he ever heard these same sounds and he said no.

It seemed that these sound waves were louder at night, and I immediately became to suspect that it had something to do with a military base nearby. Later I would learn the reason for hearing these sound was due to metal toxicity. I would also learn the detrimental effects it had on me and those around the world.

The metal fillings containing mercury, used many years ago, were designed to stop cavities. This is just one example of the causes of metal toxicity.

The World Health Organization, (WHO) identified the amalgam fillings to be the greatest source of metal toxicity to humans. There is no other source that contributes more metal toxicity than the amalgam fillings, according to the WHO.

The WHOs identification of the seriousness in metal toxicity goes against what the American Dental Association still claims as safe. Since the 1940s many physicians have stated that the mercury amalgam fillings are the biggest contributor to mental illness diseases and autism.

For more information on this interesting research please visit my resource page at ParasitesInsideMe.com.

The chemtrails that were started by the Clinton administration and continues today, have released aluminum and other toxic metals into our environment. These metals make their way down to our food, water, and the air we breathe, and are also impacting the people of the world negatively, all in the name of global warming. We are breathing and consuming more metals than our bodies can handle, and this is just one neglected topic in the world.

With the WHO admitting the massive toxicity and dangers to all people who have these fillings, shouldn't we question why the American Dental Association (ADA) has not taken the warning seriously?

Could this be why so many individuals in the world are suffering from a variety of health issues?

CHAPTER 2:
HYSTERECTOMY

Passing Massive Blood Clots

Spring was turning to summer quickly and we wanted a break from all the hard work we had been doing. We decided to take trip a to Florida for a nice long break.

I made reservations at the resort we usually stayed at and scheduled a 9-day trip to Orlando. I added two days for the drive each way, which allowed us to enjoy the journey instead of rushing. We decided to take our parents with us as they had not been on vacation for many years. The condo was big enough to fit all of us and the only added expense was food and entertainment.

We worked all day on June 1st planning to get up and leave around 3am on June 2nd. After unloading from the truck of all of our work supplies, we then loaded our luggage. We were so excited to visit with the family that we hardly got any rest.

With little sleep we headed out to make our way to Florida. The drive was hard and long. The consumption of 5-Hour energy supplements and many coffee breaks caused a 12-hour trip to be 17 not to mention we stopped to switch drivers every few hours or so.

After arriving and checking in at the resort, we unloaded the truck into the condo. We drank nasty convenience store coffee for many hours. Now we could make our delicious coffee and unwind from the drive.

It rained for much of the first 5 days of this trip so we were limited on the functions we could do. My mother had cancer many times throughout the last 25 years and would easily get sick after a trip to a different climate. Rather than risking her health, we stayed at the condo talking most of the time.

In Between the rain showers we would go visiting friends and family. My parents had gone to visit many of their cousins that they had not seen in a long time, while we would do other things. A dinner was planned for all the cousins to meet at a restaurant to eat and visit with each other. We had a lot of catching up to do and we had a great time.

Once the trip was over and we all returned home, I realized that I missed my menstrual cycle. It became a running joke that we were having a baby! At 48 years old this was not something I had even considered! I was too old, enjoying my life and my freedoms to be and do as I wish. We were almost empty nesters with only one teen left at home. Thinking about the energy it was going to take raising another baby wore me out at the thought of it.

One evening as I had just finished my nightly cup of coffee, when I stood from my seat to go to bed, I noticed my panties felt very moist. My first thought was that I had started my menstrual cycle and that I wasn't pregnant!

I went upstairs to use the bathroom and sat on the toilet when I noticed my panties were full of blood and blood clots. After looking between my legs, I saw the same image was in the toilet.

This was not coming from my bladder but instead my uterus. My initial thought is that I was pregnant and miscarrying the baby. Petrified at what I was seeing and fearing the worst, I peered around the wall while sitting on the toilet where I could see my husband lying in bed.

I politely asked if he would come to the bathroom. The sheer way I asked him was alarming enough, and I tried not to appear panicked, but needed to be assured that I was not dying.

He came to the bathroom and looked in-between my legs to see the blood was not slowing down. He could see the panic in my face and heard it in my voice and tried to assure me that I would be OK. After he positioned towels on the bed, I laid down hoping that I could calm myself down.

With fear invading my thoughts, it was hard to go to sleep this evening but eventually I did. The following morning upon waking up, I quickly jumped out of bed to see the towels I had laid on were saturated with blood, and my heart began to race.

I quickly jumped in the shower to be ready to call the OB-GYN's office, who I was sure, would have me come in. It was only 7:30am and the wait for 9am to roll around seemed like an eternity. I paced the floor and continually went to the bathroom to check on the blood flows and clots.

When 9 O'clock rolled around, I was on the phone calling the doctor's office trying to get in that same day. The young lady on the other end listened to me describe what was happening and informed me they didn't have an available opening until July 21, 2017. I was alarmed by this, as I always thought doctors held back a few appointments for emergencies. I was wrong!

Worry had taken over my mind and I became irritable and testy to my family and friends who wanted to converse with me. I was further inconsolable when I was finding no answers in my research.

Finally, the 21st arrived and we went to the office and was taken back to the exam room where Dr. GYN listened to me describe what was happening. He ordered labs, a pregnancy test, a urine test, and ultrasound. The earliest appointment for the ultrasound would not be until August 2nd at 6:30pm, a two week wait.

The pregnancy test was negative. I was not miscarrying a baby.

Fibroids Diagnosis

T he day of August 2nd had finally arrived, and I entered the facility to have the ultrasound completed which was done after-hours in the OB-GYN office. There was another woman in the waiting room ahead of me and I was praying that her examine would go quickly so I could get my test done to get the answers.

About 15-20 minutes later, I was called to the exam room and given a gown to change into. The technician began to explain the procedure that she was going to do advising me that she would insert this wand into my vagina to get pictures of my internal reproductive organs.

This is when I learned that the ultrasound techniques had changed to the use of internal wands. I was not comfortable with this new procedure and requested to utilize the older methods that I had experienced many years prior, but this was no longer an option with this facility.

As the technician began doing her scan, taking measurements and pictures, I questioned what she was seeing. She advised me that she was not permitted to disclose any findings and that she really didn't know enough to do so. My thought is that, if she didn't know what she was looking at, then how was she able to find the abnormalities?

The following day I received a call from Dr. GYN to discuss

the results of my ultrasound. He advised me that I had several uterine fibroids. I had never heard of this before and began to ask why or how this happened, but there were no clear answers. Dr. GYN wanted to schedule another appointment to discuss the options to rectify this situation. I was scheduled on September 2, 2017. More time to wait!

When the day came, my husband and I had gone into the office to see Dr. GYN. He began to explain my options, the first being a D & C to remove the fibroids. He assured me that if I selected this option, that fibroids always grow back, resulting in continued treatment. The second option was a full hysterectomy, that would eliminate the issue all together. I was not prepared to make this decision at that time. I told the doctor that I needed time to think about it. I was fearful of having a major surgery, but he assured me that I would be fine, and that it was the best option.

I know many women who have gone through this, and it didn't seem to affect them like it was me. I needed time to get my emotions in check before I could make this decision.

At this point, I had not yet connected the comments of the Dermatologist who stated the same thing about the mole coming back. My OB-GYN had just stated the same thing.

I would later question in my own thoughts how these things could grow back after being removed. There again was no clear understanding to these questions. My discovery would come in just two more years.

The Surgery

I took time to consider what the best options for me would be. I did my best to research and found no comforting answers.

Worried that I might not make it through this, I decided to find a job that offered life insurance, so I didn't leave my family in a financial bind. I had taken a job with a large grocery chain as a location Human Resources manager.

I had enormous amounts of fun performing this job, as our store had over 175 employees making every day different. I met so many wonderful people that had a positive impact in my life, which encouraged me to go back to school for my HR degree.

My menstrual cycles became irregular and very heavy, so I always had to be prepared. The cycles would last anywhere from ten to fourteen days. Each day I went to work wearing black pants to ensure any bloody mess wouldn't be noticed, nor would I visibly ruin my pants. I didn't want to be walking around with visible blood on my pants and not be aware. I also had extra pants in my truck in case I needed to change. Each month, I continued to fight my way through the heavy cycles still indecisive about the surgery.

One evening as I was working a closing shift, I sat down in my chair without thinking. I immediately felt the wetness of my pad seep through my pants and onto my seat. I quickly stood up and saw that my cloth seat was now a bloody mess. I was angry at myself for not remembering to change my pad and tampon first. I was just so busy that I had forgotten.

I quickly headed to the restroom, cleaned myself up and changed my menstrual dressings. After washing my hands, I grabbed some wet paper towels with soap and water then returned to my office to clean my chair.

Hoping no one noticed that my hands were full of paper towels, I entered my office and began to scrub my seat. Just then an employee Kim, walked into my office. Initially I was embarrassed upon her entering and her seeing my chair.

She asked me what I was doing when I began to explain what had been happening. She listened to my concerns as tears began to fall from my eyes. She was understanding and more importantly, compassionate. She was one of the employees that I had grown a nice relationship with while in this store.

After hearing my story, she began to explain that she and her daughter had experienced the same things. The massive blood loss could cause me to pass out amongst other issues. She advised me that having a full hysterectomy would be the best decision that I could make.

Listening to her story I decided that this was the best thing for me to do. It had been about 8 months since the start of this journey. Only because she shared her experiences with me, was I able to commit to the procedure. I will forever be grateful to Kim and her concern for my health. Thank you, Kim!

With my decision made, I went to see Dr. GYN and scheduled the hysterectomy for March 19, 2018. I was still worried about having this major surgery and Dr. GYN tried to put me at ease. I trusted Dr. GYN, and I knew I was in the best hands.

My surgery was scheduled for a Monday, so I started my vacation the previous day on a Sunday. I planned to return to work the following Sunday. This would give me 6 days to recover, which I felt was long enough. Taking six weeks off would be too trying for my teammates and I wouldn't want to bring hardship to them. I decided not to alert my superiors of my surgery so that I didn't have a problem returning to work. What I did on my vacation was no business of theirs.

We arrived at the hospital on the morning of my surgery and went through the check-in process. We waited in the surgery waiting area until I was called back for prepping and my husband and son would arrive shortly after.

I had a nurse whose mobile workstation was at the end of my bed where he stayed the entire time. He completed the questionnaires while we waited for my IV to be inserted.

While waiting we noticed a young lady being guided by an older lady drawing blood. She was making her way around the room coming in my direction. I told my husband that I was not allowing her to put a needle in me and he began to laugh assuring me she was. He was right, she made her way right to me.

I was not keen on having a newbie for good reason. As she approached me, I did let her know she had one shot to get it, and she blew a vein! The older lady with her took her turn, and she too blew a vein. Now I was done with these two, so my male nurse stepped in to save the day, seamlessly installing my IV in my arm and drawing blood.

It seemed like a long time before the anesthesiologist arrived but once he did, he stayed in the area about 20 minutes before knocking me out and rolling me to the operating room. The procedure was expected to take about 2 hours.

As my husband waited, he noticed the timing had surpassed the two-hour mark and became worried something was wrong. He checked in with the desk to inquire if I was OK. It took several moments to get an answer, but I was fine.

Once the procedure was completed, Dr GYN went to my husband and informed him that I was well and the reason it took longer is that I had endometriosis that had spread to my kidney, liver, intestines and sciatica nerves. The doctor informed him that he removed all that he could.

I had never been diagnosed with this before, but it didn't matter at this point, the surgery was done, and my issues were resolved. It was weird how the endometriosis had spread to all these other organs. According to the CDC studies that I have read, this was exceedingly rare.

Earlier I mentioned that I had hip and leg pain that I had endured for so many years. Post-surgery, all the pain in those areas diminished to nothing and the numbness in my butt was now gone. I hadn't realized that my butt was partially numb until after my surgery and I regained feeling.

Prior to the surgery, I had discussed the timeframe of going back to work with Dr GYN. I informed him that I walked anywhere from 6 to 10 miles per day and performed little lifting. He responded that it would help me recover quicker thereby allowing me to return to work.

Two weeks and three days after my surgery, on April 5, 2018, I went to the restroom at work and noticed that I was urinating nothing but blood. It was not coming from my vagina but my urethra. I had no symptoms of a urinary tract infection (UTI) and didn't feel ill. I felt my condition was caused from the use of a catheter during surgery. Because it was after normal business hours, I had to wait until morning to call the doctor's office.

I called the office first thing in the morning and was told to come right in that afternoon. Doctor GYN had more labs drawn and did a urine culture that showed I had a bladder infection that was gram positive. I was given antibiotics and felt like I fully recovered.

When I went back a week later for my follow-up, Dr. GYN mentioned that he wanted to do an ultrasound on my breasts for precautionary measures.

I agreed to do this, and it was scheduled for April 17th, 2018. The results came back showing several small cysts in both of my breasts. I was told there was nothing to worry about, that this was a normal occurrence in many women and didn't have the look of cancer. The doctor wasn't concerned, so I wasn't either.

With the few things that had happened it became important for me to buy a home for my family. I didn't want to die and leave them renting someone else's home. My husband and I decided that we would use the buying power of one. Meaning that we would purchase a house based on one income. This would allow the surviving spouse to live comfortably if either of us were to die.

We had our friend Amy represent us as our realtor and went to look at a few houses. None turned out to be what we wanted. We continued our search and seemed to be disappointed every time we saw a house because they always looked nicer in the pictures.

I began to express frustrations at the difficulty we had finding a home that fit the budget of one. We were not interested in marrying a mortgage that would leave the other with financial hardships. The realtor suggested we raise our purchasing price, but neither of us were willing to do that.

My husband advised me to set the notifications to be alerted for all new listings. This would give us a better chance to purchase. Not long after doing that, we would find our home situated on more than an acre. This purchase relieved me from my worries for my family.

CHAPTER 3:
NEUROLOGICAL

Heart Palpitations

After we moved into the home, our excitement was met with concern. The water in our home was brown and I was not willing to allow my family to drink that shit. We talked to the neighbors who told us that this was common until the city did a flush on the system each year. I had only heard about this kind of thing related to the issues in Flint, Michigan, but never expected this in Elizabeth City, NC.

We called a company that tested our water. Upon completion, the test results showed elevated levels of several chemicals. After hearing the results, my husband had a system installed the following day that cleared up the water, making it safe to drink.

I used the report to research the chemical compounds found in the water and was disturbed at what I found. When two specific chemicals were combined it created chloroform. Upon learning this, I called the water company to question them and found no one who could provide solid answers.

On July 31, 2018, we were holding an open house event at work. Tom, my assistant, and I were always prepared to interview regardless of an open house event. We usually had a great turn-out each week when we held our functions, and this day would be no different.

While sitting at my desk completing other tasks unrelated to the open house, my heart began to race for no apparent reason. I became lightheaded and wondered if I was having a heart attack even though I had no pain in my chest. I experienced severe light headedness and the world seemed to be turning gray and fading. I was panicking and started to pace the hallway upstairs, thinking that if I kept moving, I wouldn't pass out.

The fear of leaving my kids alone in this crazy world was not something that I could let happen just yet. I made my way to the stairs and went down and upon landing, I turned around and went back up stairs to my desk.

I was unsure what to do or if I should call 911, when Tom came out of his office to my desk. I asked him if I looked ok. He replied that I did. Then I questioned him if my eyes looked normal and again, he said they were.

He asked what was wrong and I told him what was happening. Tom being the caring person he was, directed me to go home or the hospital. I thought about it for a moment, not wanting to leave him to do all the work, but knew I needed to go the ER.

I got up from my desk and proceeded to the store manager's office. I asked if I could leave early, because I needed to go to the hospital. After mincing words with my store manager, I decided to leave regardless. My life was more important than this job.

I grabbed my things, headed to my vehicle, and got in. After I started the car, I thought, where am I going? I called the closest ER and asked if there was a long wait time. She responded that the wait was about 4 hours. This was too long, and I didn't know if they would take me back immediately or not. Then I called the hospital that was closer to my home, however it was 45 minutes away from my current location. I was told there was no wait time. This is where I decided to go. As I drove to the hospital, I wondered if I had a brain tumor or was experiencing a heart attack.

Upon arrival to the hospital, I was admitted and taken back to a room where they started the IV. Afterwards they performed an EKG showing everything was normal, then they did a chest X-ray. The radiologist noted a "Focal Density" in my left arm pit, but it was nothing to be concerned with. They said my labs were all normal but gave me Prednisone for some congestion in my chest, that I picked up from the pharmacy afterwards.

According to the National Institute of Health (NIH), imaging of the axilla (the area between the shoulder and armpit) typically occurs only when patients are symptomatic or present with newly diagnosed breast cancer.

In just over a year from now I will learn that these steroids were dangerous to my life. Not because of what the doctors knew, but because of what they didn't know. I had no idea at this point, but this would be a life changing lesson that I would have to learn.

Prednisone

I had completed my steroids and noticed the increase in symptoms as the months continued. The bottoms of my feet developed bumps under the skin causing a world of pain when I stood. It took several minutes of standing before I could walk. The severe and intense pain throughout my entire head and body began to increase.

The left side of my head began to ache constantly, along with me hearing a high-pitched buzzing in my ears. My eyes became very watery every morning, which lasted for hours, and my vision was quickly deteriorating. Brain fog appeared, prohibiting my thoughts and speech from being clear and concise. I became imbalanced and lacked coordination causing me to trip easily and drop things more frequently. Something was happening that was causing a huge disruption of my normal life.

My place of employment was an hour away but with traffic it could take me much longer to get to work. I left an hour and half prior to my scheduled time to ensure I didn't arrive late. Working a ten hour shift each day meant a 13-hour day away from a normal life. I thought maybe that the long hours had taken a toll on my body. I was getting closer to the age of 50 when everything starts to break and decided to seek another position with less demands.

I started to apply for open positions and began to make several calls to schedule interviews. One such position was with a nationwide HVAC manufacturer, and although I had no experience in this industry, I applied. I usually had good luck working in a male dominated industry and because of that, my chances were good. I had broad knowledge of the construction industry and knew I could learn this industry.

After several interviews, I was offered the store manager position, for this nationwide HVAC manufacturer. The position offered much better hours that were all daylight, Monday through Friday.

The Punctate (Brain Lesion)

I started my new position as the store manager on November 1, 2018. I was excited for the change, hoping that all of my symptoms were related to my previous long work hours and inconsistent shifts.

My new team was investing quality time in teaching me the ropes of this industry as well as their computer systems. They displayed patience with my learning and were helpful in answering all of my questions.

Derrick Earley was my customer service associate who had been with this company for 10 years. He held vast knowledge, and his patience was strong. I questioned why he wasn't the store manager. He clearly, with his knowledge, could have done the job!

His faith was strong and his voice soft when he spoke. We grew to become particularly good friends rather quickly. We talked about everything in life and how it relates to God. As time progressed, we had shared a lot about our lives including both good times and bad. There was nothing really, that we didn't discuss.

I shared with him what was happening to me and expressed that I didn't think I would live much longer. I expressed my frustration about the doctors and hospitals who could never find any real reason for my many symptoms. Derrick asked if he could pray over me, and I gladly accepted his offer even though I felt it wouldn't help.

I had prayed to my God so often that I felt that I had been rejected and forsaken. My strong faith seemed to dissipate before my eyes. My intuition seemed to be faltering to the point I didn't feel like I was receiving messages any longer. The messages would always guide me, giving me indications of the directions that I should be going in life. The messages in my dreams no longer appeared, or so I thought.

On December 8, 2018, while at work my symptoms were again alarming. Derrick once again prayed over me, and I left to go to the ER. Upon arrival, I was taken back to an exam room where the doctor ordered labs, an EKG, and a CT scan of my head w/ wo contrast. The radiologist found that I had a punctate on the frontal left lobe. This could also be classified as a brain lesion, and it was noted that I was born with it. I knew this to be false because of the many MRI's I had back in the 90's, when my PCP once suspected that I had MS. The ER doctor also said my labs had come back normal, but I knew this couldn't be right.

The gray-haired doctor in the ER arrived in my room. He seemed angry that I had made a second trip in 5 months. I was told that nothing was wrong with me except for anxiety. He proceeded to tell me that he didn't want to see me back in the ER, because it was for emergent care. He directed me to find a PCP.

I was shocked to hear this! I knew that it was emergent care, which is why I was there. I felt like I was dying and needed help. The behaviors exhibited by this doctor clearly displayed his lack of interest in discovering what was causing my symptoms.

He showed no compassion. He made me feel as though I was a bother, all the while charging me an exorbitant amount of money. More than a year later, I would find out that my labs did result, showing that I did have medical issues that were being overlooked.

Because I had just been told not to come back, I worried about needing to go back to that hospital again. I began to wonder if they were allowed to refuse me medical treatment, so I started to research it. I learned that they are NOT allowed to refuse me, but what if they purposely failed to help me?

As I began to search for a PCP, I knew my first choice was Dr. Eldon Beard, but he was 6 hours away. Working Monday through Friday and being so new in my position, it would not be appropriate to ask for time off through the week. This prevented me from obtaining treatment and compassion from Dr. Beard at that time.

I called many doctors' offices nearby and none were taking new patients. It would take me a couple of weeks to find a doctor to help manage my health issues. I finally found Dr. PCP and made my first appointment. During this appointment, he stated that he felt my issues stemmed from anxiety.

The last ER doctor called my condition "anxiety" and I felt this was peculiar how he was saying the same thing. Yes, I was having anxiety but why? It didn't seem that there was any interest to investigate the cause of the symptoms, but instead just treat them. He prescribed Zoloft to treat my symptoms. He also had Dr. GI contact me to schedule a colonoscopy for late January 2019.

I accepted the Zoloft he prescribed me in hopes that the doctors were right. It did help calm me down, but it did not resolve my issues.

Derrick, and I continued to pray and believe that God would help me through this phase of my life. His faith had encouraged me to revisit my relationship with God because I came to question if there was a God, and if there was why had he forsaken me? I couldn't imagine why he would allow me to suffer to this extent. Not only would I discover over the next year that God was always there, but I would also discover his plan for my life.

I began to wonder if I had gotten sick from the brown city water provided to our home. I even wondered if I had contracted food poisoning but didn't know that if I did whether or not it could last for months.

Later when I received my medical records, I concluded that the doctors either didn't look at my labs, they didn't know what they were looking at or refused to acknowledge the results. My lab work showed my lymphocytes were low at 17, my absolute Eosinophil were high at a 6, my urine specific gravity was low at 1.003. At every visit to any doctor, my labs always resulted, but each time I was told that they were normal. My teeth started breaking, I woke up grinding my teeth and having fists that were clenched. I was gaining weight at an alarming rate. My legs were restless causing me an urge to stretch them. When I would stretch, I would have a muscle pull in the left side of my back.

The stress of this unknown illness was taking a toll on me and my family. I lost interest in regular activities and people in general. I had little energy to do small chores around the house and had to push myself to go to work. I look back and see just how relentless I was and grateful because this was how my parents had raised us to be.

Determined, I continued to see doctors and began to experience their gaslighting and poor treatment. I was adamant that someone was going to help me one way or another. This was a "John Q" awakening for me, referencing the movie starring Denzel Washington. That movie is certainly a correct depiction of western medicine. I know there are exceptionally good doctors out there; I just wasn't finding them.

Each night I could feel my blood pressure drop exceptionally low and would check the veins on my hands to see them disappear. I would jump out of the bed, trying to raise my blood pressure and when it didn't work, I went into a full panic attack. Whatever I was fighting, it seemed I was losing the battle.

Many nights I went to bed unsure if I would wake up the next morning. Each night I grabbed my bible and held it to my head as I prayed then tucked it under my pillow, in belief that my God would save me.

My fear of dying during the night, only to have my son find me in the morning, made me leave my flashlight on. This offered both comfort and assurance that I would wake up. The darkness of night left me feeling the most vulnerable to die.

My confidence and self-esteem were on a steep decline, further removing my passion to make a positive impact on peoples lives. The once uplifting person I tried to be was now fading into darkness. Everything about me was changing into something I didn't like.

My emotional state became elevated to constant crying, fear, and worry. I had lost complete control over my life with no one to understand me. The devastation of increasing medical expenses was nothing short of a nightmare. The more money I wasted experiencing medical gaslighting, the more pissed I became.

My spirit was being broken which had not ever happened before. Deep down in my soul, I knew I had better find my fight because I was going to need it. I was always the fighter in the family, the one that fixed problems for my children, now it was all I could do to breathe. I always stood up for those who couldn't stand up for themselves. Now suddenly, it seemed I was the one who needed someone to fight for me, but who would this be?

Several months prior we had taken a rescue dog that was about to be euthanized in August 2018. The animal shelter could not find anyone to take her, so we did. I really did not have an interest in taking another rescue, but this little girl's soul was broken, and I knew what that felt like and I knew we could help her. I thought she needed me, but quickly discovered that it was I who needed her.

While lying in bed one evening she came over to my stomach and shoved her nose into my abdomen and started sniffing. She would sniff then stop and look at me. She had done this several times. Both she and my Yorkie had both done this to the left side of my forehead that same night. I worried that she was trying to tell me that I had stomach and brain cancer. The actions she and the Yorkie displayed made it obvious they were trying to alert me to something. The Yorkie we have had since 2010 had never done this prior.

Only days afterwards, I was awakened at 3am from a nightmare of parasites having invaded my body. I had never seen parasites in my life, but the images were truly clear, showing dozens and dozens of them throughout my stomach. The images I saw, were as though I were inside my body seeing the many worms. Horrified at this dream, I could not go back to sleep that night. I couldn't imagine why I would have had a nightmare such as this. I didn't know anything about parasites nor did the thought ever enter my mind. This dream, I will remember, until the day I die.

As time passed, I had found it increasingly difficult to breathe at night. I had to train my brain to mechanically force my lungs to move in and out. I would stop breathing many times throughout each night and wake up gasping for air. The forced action became a normal routine of practice every night prior to going to sleep. I had to fight to survive to ensure I didn't hurt the hearts of my children. I was doing this for them because I wasn't done teaching them and ensuring myself, that they had the skills to survive this nutty world.

Nodule

I decided to reach out to a couple doctors who we knew on a personal level to ask for assistance. I hated to ask for help from friends and acquittances, but I was out of choices as my life was on the line. On January 5, 2019, I sent a text to Dr. A. to ask her if she could help guide me as to what could be wrong with me.

Dr. A had advised me that I should go back to the ER and have them check my carotid arteries in my neck for any blockages. I had to think about which hospital to go to since the last visit to the E-City hospital, the doctor told me he didn't want to see me in there again. I didn't really want to drive to Chesapeake and do that longer drive. I decided to hell with it, I am going to the closest facility.

I left the house and headed to the E-City ER once again to find the same doctor who told me not to return. There was also a nurse practitioner who was doing all the work and I was glad to see him walk through the door of my room. The nurse started the EKG and inserted the IV into my arm while I began to explain my symptoms to the NP. I told him what our doctor friend had advised, which was why I was there.

The nurse interrupted and stated that my symptoms sounded like thyroid issues. This was an interesting statement since no doctor had mentioned this prior. The NP ordered a CT scan of my neck and labs.

With the IV installed, blood drawn, I was then taken to radiology where the scan was performed on my neck. It was found that I had a thyroid nodule 2cm big. It was now apparent that the nurse was right! Maybe she should be the doctor!

The lab work showed Neutrophils high @ 76; Lymphocytes low @17; urine specific gravity high @ 1.060 and again I was told by the NP that my labs were all good. How could there be nothing wrong when the labs are showing abnormalities? Errors in reading my reports as well as ill-advising me would continue to happen in the future.

I received my diagnosis and was discharged from the ER. I called my husband to inform him of my new diagnosis. Finally, I was getting answers to the potential causes of my symptoms.

Since this was over the weekend, I had to wait until Monday to call my PCP. On Monday, I called to schedule an appointment to get a referral to an Endocrinologist. I was scheduled for the following day, January 8, 2019.

I arrived at the office and was taken back to the exam room. A young nurse came in to perform the normal check-in procedures. She asked me how I was doing, and I told her I was not happy about this recent finding of a thyroid nodule and was curious why Dr. PCP didn't recognize or investigate the symptoms I had experienced.

After the nurse completed taking my vitals, she said the doctor would be in shortly. I let her know that I did not really need to see him I just needed a referral to an endocrinologist. She left the room and returned to let me know that the doc would be making my referral and would call with an appointment. A few days afterwards, I received a call from the endocrinologist's office to schedule an appointment for January 24, 2019.

A few days prior to the appointment, I received a phone call from Dr. Endo, the endocrinologist, to discuss what would take place at this appointment. I was told that they would be doing a needle aspiration on my thyroid to try to decipher if it was cancerous. I had not heard of this procedure prior to this conversation but I would at a minimum, call my sister to have her explain it to me.

My husband had taken the day off from work to attend this appointment with me. Upon arrival and check-in, we were taken back to the procedure room. The doctor was in the room awaiting our arrival and explained the process to us. Once I agreed, he retrieved staff members to assist him in completing the procedure.

I got up on the table with the large light glaring into my eyes and my husband next to me. I grabbed his hand for security and comfort. The doctor began his probing of my thyroid with a total of six needles. I did well until the last needle prick when I became emotional, and the tears started flowing. The procedure was completed, and we headed back to our home an hour away.

A few days later we received the results that were inconclusive for cancer. The doctor recommended that I have the left lobe of my thyroid removed. He said that if it was cancer, it was the best to have and easiest to cure. He recommended two surgeons. I was not familiar with either of these referrals and decided that I would go with my own surgeon.

Dr. Surgeon was a doctor who had previously cared for a loved one, removing a goiter in 1997. He had decades of experience with this type of surgery and was the one that I wanted to perform my procedure.

For the previous 6 months, I had experienced extreme fatigue and found it difficult to stay awake. Working everyday became harder and harder but I still didn't miss any work. Once I got home and entered the house, I would fall into the recliner too exhausted to take off my coat. I would sleep for hours until my husband would wake me up to go to bed.

The pain throughout my body continued to increase along with my weight. I didn't have an appetite and ate very little each day. I had severe acid reflux that seemed worse when I consumed water and made me want to rip my esophagus out of my body.

As events unfolded related to my health, my anger began to grow to unreasonable levels. I was angry at my husband for not helping me in this fight with the medical industry. I was angry at the doctors for being so careless with my health issues as well as their lack of compassion. I was angry at God for allowing this to happen to me. I was just angry at everyone and everything.

I had to learn that I was in control of my destiny, even if it meant I had to go it alone. I had to remove all the outside emotional influences and focus on getting myself back to optimal health. Even my family would have to be put to the side. This would prove to be the most difficult and expensive task I have ever done in my life. What was to come, will shock and will not be for the faint hearted. The anger that I felt at this time would prove to be trivial compared to the anger that was to come.

CHAPTER 4: APPENDECTOMY

Hospital Visit

I had been sleeping in the spare bedroom on January 15, 2019, when I woke up around 11:30pm. The pain that hit me felt as though I were being stabbed in my stomach. I got out of bed panicked and started to pace the floor crying, trying to figure out what I should do. I had been to the hospitals 3 times, the doctor's office several times and no one had found anything outside of the nodule; surely that wasn't causing the grueling abdominal pains.

My husband heard me crying, pacing the floor, and got out of bed. He tried to calm me down, but I wasn't having any of it because he didn't understand. It seemed as no one understood the level of pain I had. I told my husband I was going to the hospital in Chesapeake and that I needed to reach out to Dr. Z to see if he was working.

My husband wanted to take me, but I refused as I didn't want to awaken our son. In the past when I had gone to the ER, they never really did anything but charge me a lot of money and never really figured out what was going on with me.

My husband contacted Dr. Z to see if he was working that night and to let him know of my symptoms. Dr. Z was not working, however he called the hospital staff to alert them that I was en route.

After I arrived at the ER and was checked in, I was taken back for evaluation. They hooked me up to the monitors and IV and in a brief time I was taken to radiology for an abdominal CT scan. The EKG test indicated that there was nothing wrong with my heart, but we all know that EKG testing is not accurate.

According to ScienceDaily, a study done including 500 patients, showed inaccuracies in false positive results, at rates between 77 and 82%. It also showed that the false negative results were 6 and 7%. Knowing this, I question whether the testing is simply for billable profitable purposes.

The scan showed calcified gallstones in my gallbladder with thickening of the wall. My appendix was enlarged measuring 10mm. There were small irregular calcifications within the appendix. Stomach and bowel findings were unremarkable meaning there were no abnormalities noted. My white blood count was elevated, and I was given nothing to assist me with fighting my infection.

I was asked to return to my PCP doc in order to decide my next steps. I left the hospital and went straight to work, arriving only a few minutes late. While I was on my break, I called Dr. PCP to schedule an appointment. In a few days, I would have the opportunity to discuss my newly identified medical issues. I was starting to make some headway.

Emergency Surgery

As I waited for my PCP appointment, my pain continued to intensify greatly. Only two days after my diagnosis of appendicitis and gallstones, I was awakened from sleep on January 18, 2019. I was unsure if my appendix had ruptured but knew the pain was indicative of this possibility.

 I got out of bed just as I had 2 nights prior and again started to pace the floor feeling helpless. We repeated the same scenario as we had just a couple of nights previously. My husband, who had only been home for a few hours, tried to calm me down. I sent a text to Dr. Z to let him know that I was enroute back to the hospital.

Once again, I went through the check in process and was taken back to a room within just a few minutes. The encounter with the nurses this night would expose their real personalities and lack of compassion.

The nurse who entered the room to insert the IV had done a terrible job. The needle felt as though it had gone through my vein causing pain in my entire lower arm. I had complained about this to the nurse who then rolled her eyes, patted the IV and said it was fine. So much for listening to the patient, I guess.

Shortly afterwards a radiology tech had come to take me to do another CT scan. I advised him that I felt like the needle had been inserted improperly. As I was explaining this to the radiology tech, the nurse had come back into the room clearly agitated that I was complaining to the tech. After we arrived at the radiology dept, the tech removed the IV and reinserted it in my other arm without event and eliminating my discomfort.

Throughout the early morning hours, they did several different scans as noted below:

The first test done was an **X-Ray of the chest preformed at 4:41am.** This report noted my lungs were clear and everything was normal.

The second test done was a CT of the chest at 4:59am. No Correlation: noting the following:

Mild degenerative changes of the spine; atelectasis right lung base (collapsed lung or area of lung); thyroid unremarkable; gallstone; and appendix measures 12cm.

Correlation: Non-Contrast CT scan; There is a gallstone. Liver, spleen, pancreas, adrenal glands, kidneys, bladder, and adnexa are unremarkable. Uterus is absent. Colon and terminal ileum are unremarkable. Appendix measures 12cm. There are appendicoliths (calcified deposit within the appendix). No surrounding inflammation.

Another CT scan of my abdomen and pelvis was completed at 5:10am. This scan resulted in the following: liver, spleen, pancreas, adrenal glands, kidneys, bladder, and adnexa are unremarkable. Correlation: Non-Contrast CT scan 1/16/2019 Findings: appendix measuring 12cm. There are appendicoliths, small amounts of free fluid in the pelvis, suggestive of appendicitis. 12cm dilation of the appendix with appendicoliths; atelectasis right lung base.; thyroid was unremarkable; there is a gallstone; gallbladder wall measure 2mm. Sonographic Murphy sign is negative; right kidney measures 11.2x4.1x4.8cm. Mild 8 cm common bile duct dilatation.

There was no mention of the newly diagnosed thyroid nodule on any of the scans or x-rays that they did. How was that possible when the other hospital did diagnose a nodule in my thyroid?

A little while later the attending physician arrived to disclose that my appendix had grown 2cm in two days and that it likely had to come out. He stated that he had called for a surgeon who would arrive a little while later.

Dr. Surgeon arrived sometime later, entered my room and sat down. He too explained that my appendix had grown 2cm since my scan two days prior and said that it needed to come out. He stated that my WBC were elevated but felt it was related to my appendix. There was one more test he performed, an ultrasound of the appendix to gain a better understanding prior to my surgery. He stated that my gallbladder had to come out as well but could not be done at the same time.

I sent a text to my husband to inform him that I was going to have surgery. He went ahead and got our son out of bed and the two of them headed to the hospital.

The young ultrasound technician came to retrieve me for the last test. She was not interested in small talk as we entered the room to complete my scan. While doing the scan, I noticed she started on the right side near my appendix, even though my pain was on the left side. I asked her about it, and she seemed irked that I would even inquire. With an angry inflection in her tone, she began to explain that the pain in my right side would radiate to my left side. Her explanation failed to resonate with any logic to me.

Once my labs and ultrasound results were back, Dr. Surgeon came to my room. He explained to me and my family what was going to take place during my procedure.

Following are the results of my labs at that time, clearly showing I was having more issues than what was addressed. My liver function was low indicating function issues but was never disclosed to me at that time or ever. This is why it is important to obtain a copy of all medical records and study them for one's own knowledge.

The overall WBC @ 15.5; MPV was high @ 11.0; Neutrophils were high @ 85.00; Lymphocytes low @ 7.8; Glucose was high @ 113; SGOT was low @ 11; Bilirubin high @ 1.1; albumin low @ 3.3.

Shortly thereafter, my husband and son arrived at the hospital. I was already in pre-op area awaiting my turn for the surgery. After waiting about an hour, they took me back to the surgery room but didn't knock me out, causing me to be more nervous than I already was. After several minutes, the anesthesiologist positioned my mask and directed me to take a deep breath. I was out like a light.

I was awakened after surgery as I was being moved to a regular room in the hospital. My husband and son were already in the room waiting for my arrival. As I became more coherent, I lifted my gown to look at my incisions and immediately noticed that my torso had become disfigured. The five incisions were covered with gauze.

My lower pelvis area was flat, however my upper abdomen stuck out. I also had an extraordinarily strong sensation of something inside me, squeezing me. It felt like I had a rubber band or belt inside my waist. My stomach being separated at the location of this belt like feeling. Imagine a rubber band going around your waist being tight, causing a separation of the abdomen. That is exactly what my stomach looked like. It still does two and half years later. At the time, I wasn't sure if this was a side effect of my surgery.

Dr. Surgeon came to my room a couple of hours later to check on me. I had addressed my concern over the appearance of my stomach and the tightness that I felt. He informed me that it was swelling and would take some time to diminish. He also mentioned that my gallbladder issues could be causing some of the swelling. I wasn't so sure about this because my stomach did not look like this prior to this surgery.

The following day, I was released from the hospital. My husband took me home and got me situated on the couch before he went to pick up my meds. I was prescribed Percocet prior to my release but decided not to take it. I still had plenty of the Tramadol left from the hysterectomy 9 months earlier, so I opted to take those as needed. I took a total of 5 throughout the two-week post-surgery period. I was directed to take 2 weeks off from work until I had my post-op follow-up visit.

As the medicines from the hospital wore off, the tight feeling that I had around my waste became even more apparent. I also noticed that I could not empty my colon, but related that to the surgery. After looking in the mirror naked, I noticed that I had two fatty pouches just above both of my legs in my pelvic area. Again, I attributed this to swelling since the doc made 5 holes throughout my abdomen for my appendectomy. At each of my incision points there was a bulge. I had a large protrusion in my epigastric area and by the incision that was made by my liver. My body no longer looked the same as it always had and I was disgusted at what I saw. To date, I still have five remaining bulges displaying a deformity in my abdomen.

January 29, 2019, I arrived for my post op visit with Dr. Surgeon and pointed out the distention in my upper abdomen. I explained that I felt a tightness inside where my abdomen was visibly separated. I expressed the difficulty that I was having in voiding my colon. This time, I was told it could take a few months of healing time before the swelling would go down. He also advised me to take fiber to help with the excretory processes. I accepted his reasoning because he was the doctor.

I returned to work the following day with lifting restrictions. The bad abdominal pains had diminished and I was incredibly happy about that. The fiber was failing to assist me in passing any stool and seemed to be exacerbating the situation. The only thing new happening was that I started excessively passing gas. I contributed that to the air that they fill you with during surgeries. For now, I had to be grateful that my issues were being rectified.

My colonoscopy that was scheduled for late January had to be cancelled due to this surgery.

Nodule Testing

Now that my appendectomy was taken care of, it was time to focus on my thyroid issues.

My first appointment with Dr. Ham was scheduled for February. It had been decades since I had seen the doctor who had previously cared for a loved one. I knew this doctor was an excellent surgeon and had great bedside manners. He was compassionate about what he did and performed outstanding work.

My daughter and I arrived at the office for my appointment, and I was incredibly nervous about having any part of my thyroid removed. Because it was very close to major arteries, I wanted to ensure I had the best surgeon for this procedure.

Dr. Ham entered the room stating that he had looked at all of my records online and he saw how much I had gone through lately. This taught me that our records are all online which I never knew, nor do I agree with. This made me feel like we have been bamboozled by our government to believe we have privacy rights under HIPPA. As I was going from doctor to doctor everything regarding my medical records was visible to all of them.

Dr. Ham asked how we found him, and I told him that he had cared for a loved one years prior. I explained that I had received two surgeon referrals from my endocrinologist, but I was not familiar with either doctor and decided to go with him. His response was that of confusion as he stated he didn't understand that because the doctors were all in the same group.

Dr. Ham began to explain the situation with my nodule and the chances of it being cancerous. He wasn't concerned since thyroid cancer rarely spreads elsewhere in the body. He agreed that it needed to be removed but not until he had one more test completed. My daughter and I had asked a lot of questions related to the safety of this surgery. He answered our questions and assured us both that everything would be fine.

The testing facility turned out to be minutes from my place of work which was perfect because I could use my lunch hour to complete it. I scheduled the test and after check-in, was taken back to the exam room. There was a large machine in this very cold space, but it was not intimidating. The technician explained that this machine would swirl all around me as the testing was taking place. She had inserted an IV and then the iodine to implement the testing which took about an hour.

The results came back rather quickly indicating a cold nodule. A cold nodule does not produce thyroid hormones and a hot nodule produces excess thyroid hormones. A cold nodule up-takes less iodine and a hot nodule takes up more iodine. In my thinking, the nodule is not utilizing the same blood system since it did not up-take any of the iodine. In hindsight as I analyze all of my events, I believe that my nodule had its own blood system, since it would not uptake the iodine. This confirms for me, that what was being referred to as a "nodule" was in fact a "parasitic cyst."

Later, after learning that Iodine kills parasites, I had begun to question, whether the iodine that came through the IV had killed many of my intestinal parasites. It was 8 months after my appendectomy that I would discover another potential cause of my multiple illnesses. After seeing parasites in my stools, it was certainly something to consider and discuss.

Now that all the testing was done, we know cancer is possible and the nodule was a cold. Dr. Ham's office had scheduled a pre-op appointment with me to discuss the Iodine test results and what to expect after surgery. The surgery was then scheduled for March 28, 2019.

Lobectomy

My husband had come home for the procedure to take me to the hospital and on March 28, we reported to the surgery center. I had one of the best nurses I had seen up to this point. The nurse expertly installed my IV causing no pain, which was a first for me. Dr. Ham stopped by to say hello and to let us know that I would be taken back for the procedure very briefly. It was only about 15 minutes before I was retrieved, knocked out and taken in for surgery.

After the surgery, I was awakened upon being transferred to a new bed in my room. There my family was, once again waiting for me. It wasn't long after when Dr. Ham had stopped in to check on me and let us know that my surgery was a success. He would inform us of my pathology results after testing had been completed.

The nurses at this hospital in VA Beach were nice and the facility more accommodating compared to the other hospitals that I had been treated in over the last several months. Every room had a couch in the room, making it more accommodating and relaxing for visitors.

My incision and the drain tube were surrounded with gauze to catch the fluids at the base of my neck. I was petrified to look at the incision or the tube, so I avoided the mirror. On the following day I grew the courage to look at my incisions. Initially this was alarming for me to view, however I quickly became acclimated.

By that afternoon, I started to feel a little under the weather as though I had an infection. I paged for the nurse and upon her arrival I asked for antibiotics explaining that I had an infection. She advised me that I had to wait until the doctor came around but that wasn't going to work for me. I requested that she find and bring the doctor to my room. Infections can grow to be massive killers and that I wasn't going to wait for it to kill me.

She turned around after completing her tasks and left the room. It was about 40 minutes later or thereabouts when she returned with the doctor. I explained that I could feel an infection and that I needed antibiotics. The doctor said she needed to get some lab work to confirm this and proceeded to tell me that the previous lab work showed an elevated white blood count of 17 which shows an infection, but they still needed another test done. I responded that "one way or another" they were going to give me antibiotics that I was not going to let them kill me.

I had an issue with her statement, they already knew I had an infection? And yet they failed to treat my infection? How is this even legal, they are aware of an issue and fail to rectify it?

The nurse and doctor left, with the nurse returning to draw blood for testing. After about an hour or so, the doctor returns and proceeds to tell me that my white blood count had increased to 21, and they were going to administer IV antibiotics. I continued the IV therapy the rest of that day, and the following day until they released me. I had no further incidents with infections at that time.

I went back to work that following Monday with restrictions similar to those that I received with my hysterectomy and appendectomy. I was not taking any pain meds because I had no pain from this surgery. After the removal of the left lobes of my thyroid I noticed a change in my symptoms. My lightheadedness has subsided to a great degree, and I was able to drive with no concerns. My heart rate abnormalities had disappeared altogether. I regained my ability to make sound decisions once again and the confusion I had experienced for too long had dissipated into thin air.

Bodily Changes

Three surgeries had been completed in the last year with only one remaining. Dr. Surgeon informed me that I had to wait 1.5 to 2 months before removing my gallbladder. This would push my surgery date to at least the end of June. I was feeling better than I had in a long time, and had more energy as well.

Since my appendectomy I had been unable to empty my bowels, and my upper stomach started to grow where it was separated from top to bottom at my waistline. I had a rash all over my abdomen and had used different topical creams, but nothing brought me any relief.

I informed several doctors about my stomach issues and my inability to void my bowels. I was however repeatedly told nothing was wrong with me. Dr Surgeon must have been right that my gallbladder was causing these issues although I wasn't so sure about this assertion since my deformity appeared after my appendectomy.

As the months progressed, my breasts increased in volume and became very itchy. I still had the body aches and pains throughout my legs, shoulders, and arms however the intensity was growing.

I returned to see Dr. Surgeon regarding the increased volume of my abdomen, and he assured me that it was related to my gallbladder. Knowing that interns and nurses, may at times perform some of the medical tasks during surgeries, I asked him if anyone other than himself had executed any part of my procedure during my surgery. I was interested to find out if an intern had performed anything on me and I was told no.

I had been taking Dulcolax and was still taking the Metamucil to help with my constipation issue that I had been experiencing since my appendectomy. I was not having favorable results expelling any stool but instead the recommended protocols seemed to block me up even more.

The dangers of taking Dulcolax on a long-term basis can cause many issues within the intestines. Because polyethylene glycol, an oil based ingredient, causes an exorbitant amount of subsequent medical issues. I know this because of my experience. I had dried blood specs throughout my stools, but I didn't understand why at this point. In my soul, I felt that Dr. Surgeon had lacerated my intestines and sutured it into one of the incisions. I continued to believe this was the cause of my stomach separation and pain.

May 2019, I went back to my PCP complaining about the significant changes in my stomach. I explained that additionally, I was experiencing a painful belt like feeling inside me like a squeezing sensation. Dr. PCP ordered another CT scan of my abdomen.

I arrived at the hospital in Chesapeake and upon signing into radiology I was handed a clipboard with a questionnaire. This form had a diagram of the body to indicate the areas of concern. After notating that "this was the result of surgery" I went on to indicate my problem areas again commenting that, in my opinion, this situation was caused from and the result of my surgery. I had no proof of this but was going off my intuition. With no evidence that Dr. Surgeon had injured me, I was left to believe that my gallbladder was causing this dysentery, disfigurement, and my constipation.

I waited more than eight weeks to have my gallbladder removed. My procedure was scheduled on August 12, 2019. The pain that I had was different than the stabbing pains that I had experienced earlier in the year. I would surely be able to tell, after this last surgery whether or not my current issues were caused by my gallbladder.

It was astonishing to me that I had already experienced the loss of 3 organs and was about to endeavor into a 4th. All of this happened in such a brief period of time without anyone ever questioning why. This was far from normal by any standards and I was puzzled as to how this could happen. There were no answers just yet, but soon enough, the discovery will be made, and the dots will all connect.

CHAPTER 5: GALL BLADDER

Surgery

T he morning of August 12, 2019, my husband and I had arrived at the hospital in Chesapeake for my gallbladder surgery. After check-in we were sent to the pre-op waiting area until they took me back and then brought my husband to my room.

We waited about an hour before the anesthesiologist came by and completed his questionnaire and then took me back to perform my out-patient procedure and knocked me out.

After the surgery I was awakened in post op recovery with a nurse yelling at me. I felt extremely fatigued and unable to wake up. I just wanted to sleep. The nurse continued to yell telling me to take a deep breath but it was too hard. He continued until I followed his commands. I faintly remember him talking to someone but was too tired to even pay attention. I couldn't open my eyes. At some point the anesthesiologist pulled me up from a lying position and began to talk to me. I don't remember what he was saying, but I do remember asking what to do if it happened again in which, he told me to call 911. I was released from the hospital afterwards but don't remember much of what happened.

According to the records I would obtain later, it was clear that I crashed hard in post-op observations. At no time did any doctor report this to my husband who was waiting for me, nor did they tell me when I was free of influence of anesthesia or pain meds. One would think that this vital information should be communicated to my spouse and referenced at a minimum for any future surgeries. Even at my post-op visit with my doctor, I was never informed of this important event.

It was clear in my records that the medical team worked hard to get my BP to stabilize. Several times there was no measurement, indicating that my heart had stopped. This information was only discovered AFTER I obtained copies of my records. During a discussion with another doctor, I was informed that medically speaking, it was obvious that my heart had stopped.

My blood pressure reading at 12:23, 12:26, 13:16, and 13:17 PM indicates no blood pressure measurement. This means that my heart had stopped, and the measurement is a zero. My medical report is included here for reference purposes.

BP 73/46; MAP 52 PULSE 54 @ 12:18pm **100mcg OF NEO ADMINISTERED**

BP 92/39; MAP 53 PULSE 42 @ 12:20PM **EPINEPHRINE 5MG ADMINISTERED.**

BP ---; MAP 71 PULSE 43 @ 12:23PM

BP --; MAP 54 PULSE 60 @ 12:26PM

BP 88/50; MAP 60 PULSE 58 @ 23:35PM DR NOTIFIED

BP 150/70; MAP 89 PULSE 43 @ 12:41PM **20MG EPINEPHRINE ADMINISTERED RESPONDED**

BP 154/53; MAP 74 PULSE 53 @ 12:46PM

BP 133/51; MAP 69 PULSE 59 @ 12:50PM

BP 140/48; MAP 73 PULSE 53 @ 13:00PM

BP 102/43; MAP 57 PUSE 54 @ 13:15PM

BP -- --; MAP – PULSE 42 @ 13:16PM 20MG EPINEPHRINE ADMINISTERED RESPONDED

BP --; MAP – PULSE 53 @ 13:17PM

I have more questions surrounding this event than I have answers. How could they have released me, if my last blood pressure reading was nothing? There were several incidents recorded indicating my low blood pressure, pulse, and MAP readings. Only one minute after my last dose of Ephedrine, my charts no longer have any further readings.

It wouldn't be until I got my medical records that I discovered in the surgical notes that Dr. Surgeon had found omental tissue, in the same area of the previous incision he made. It was noted that he cut it away. This is indicative of the incisional hernia that would take more than a year to get diagnosed on a CT scan. Why would he fail to tell me that?

Recovery

I had good and bad days after my gallbladder removal and followed another six weeks of restrictions. I was confused about how much had taken place in such a brief period of time. No one questioned any of it, but instead made me feel as if I were a hypochondriac. I asked myself why it would take so many CT scans and visits to my doctors to find a thyroid nodule, appendicitis, or gall stones? We spent an incredible amount of money trying to get answers up to this point. What I did not know was that this was just the beginning of a nightmare.

I needed to understand why my body had broken down so quickly with so many issues in such a brief time. I requested my medical records for which the hospital charged me $175.00 US for copies. Hospitals are allowed to charge patients for copies of their records even though the patients have been charged thousands of dollars for services rendered. You would think that a copy of medical records would be freely provided upon release. Why did I have to request my records, by calling, completing a release form, paying for the records, then physically picking them up?

After I received my 800+ pages of medical records from one hospital, I noticed that the pathology reports stated that I had no gallstones. The CT scans showed their presence on more than one occasion. It then became a question as to what the radiologists actually saw and how they could have been wrong. Or was it the pathology department who had been incompetent?

What happens next will devastate me to the brink of unimaginable emotional and physical turmoil that would bring me to my knees. The events that will transpire over the next 7 months is (in my opinion) criminal and may shock you as much as it did me. The events will shake me to my core and test my will to survive. This will be the most monumental challenge that I have ever faced in my life.

I was healing nicely and had felt that my condition had improved compared to my previous months of agony. I was hopeful and relieved that I made it through the many surgeries that I had encountered.

During my 6-week post op visit with Dr. Surgeon, I explained that my stomach was hurting in a way that felt as though my esophagus was being strangled, differently than before, and I believed it to be the result of the dysentery of my abdomen. I continued to tell him that the recommended Dulcolax and MiraLAX had not improved my constipation. I lifted my shirt, showing him my stomach while explaining that this was not normal.

My stomach which had grown sizeably since my appendectomy was still growing increasingly larger and getting harder. I looked like a child from Ethiopia with the large center of my stomach being distended. I had pain in my ascending, transverse, and descending colon areas. The uncomfortable tight belt feeling that went around my waist remained.

This time I was told that it could take months for the swelling to go down. It looked as though I was near the end of a pregnancy and ready to pop.

Brain Lesion

My husband and I got up on a Saturday morning, and were enjoying our coffee and some quiet time together. My husband was sitting at the breakfast bar, and I was seated in my recliner. Out of nowhere I suddenly became severely dizzy. The more I moved my head the worse it got, and I started to panic as I had so many times before.

I told my husband that I needed to go to the ER. He quickly helped me get to our car and raced me to the hospital in E-City. Immediately, I was transported to a room and hooked up to an IV saline solution. An EKG was also performed. Just as quickly, blood was drawn and I was taken back for a CT scan of my brain. The staff were unusually kind on this visit, and I relate that to my husband being present. Every other time that I was in the ER, I had been alone and the demeanor of the staff was both unprofessional and discriminatory.

We waited for the results to arrive to discover that I now had a brain lesion on my left frontal lobe, measuring 2cm. Now if you remember I had a previous scan on December 8, 2018, where it was noted that I had a punctate on my left frontal lobe. This means that it grew in size and was given a new name.

The radiologist noted that it was nothing of a serious nature, however the doctor was referring me to a neurologist. The kicker was that the doctor that they referred me to was 4.5 hours away! This felt like punishment, I was treated so poorly for several months and now was being referred to a doctor who was so far away. I experienced gaslighting and rolling of the eyes from the professionals, which was a normal routine of behavior coming from them. This was just another level of unreasonable treatment. I was prescribed motion sickness pills to help with my dizziness which we picked up at Walmart on our way back home. I took the meds as prescribed, however I saw zero improvement.

My husband had a friend who once battled with vertigo. He educated him on ear crystals and how they can and do work themselves loose. I was sent some videos on the steps to take to realign my ear crystals and get them back into place. When I got home from work, I pulled up the videos, following along with the instructions as it played. I was amazed that when I got up, I was no longer dizzy. I later learned that antibiotics, medicines and even illness can cause ear crystals to become displaced. The video displayed was that of two chiropractors performing the movements demonstrating the realignment of ear crystals.

This leads me to more questions. None of the doctors that I had seen mentioned ear crystals, why was that? Did they know about this realignment technique? Why were they not performing it? Why were they instead prescribing more pharmaceuticals? Why not fix the problem?

Colonoscopy

My stomach continued to swell after my gallbladder removal along with increased pain and weight. The only responses I got from my doctors was that nothing was wrong, however they recommended that I had to lose weight. Losing weight was not an option since my food intake was minimal eating only once a day. It wasn't like I was sitting around eating bon bons all day. I still tried to stay active even as I continued to grow weaker, experiencing less energy. At some point I thought the alarm bells would go off triggering some investigations as to why all these things were taking place, but I was wrong.

I was unable to eat by October of 2019. Food felt like it could not pass to my stomach, staying in my neck, causing me to feel like I was choking. I was reduced to eating only 1 yogurt a day for a month and a half. My husband purchased a box of Boost, a nutritional supplement allowing me to maintain adequate levels of dietary nutrition.

Prior to my appendectomy, I had a colonoscopy scheduled in Jan 2019. My paperwork had been completed for my colonoscopy at that time, but the appendectomy delayed this procedure. It was time to get it done.

I called Dr. Colon's office to reschedule my colonoscopy procedure, which was scheduled for November 19, 2019. I updated my medical records reflecting my most recent surgeries. The open-access coordinator was amazed at the many medical events that had taken place in such a brief time. Outside of that there were no additional changes made to my health history records. There were absolutely NO questions related to mental health on the paperwork that I submitted.

My doctor's office called to inform me that they had called my prescriptions for the cleansing products into the pharmacy. I received an emailed list of directions for taking this concoction for 3 days prior to my procedure. The medicines prescribed were intended to empty out my bowels completely. I picked these up after work and went home.

Upon arriving home, I went to see my neighbor Jackie, we discussed a member of her family who had recently had the coloscopy procedure. Curious, I asked what prescription was recommended for their procedure. I was told that their doctor had prescribed Gatorade with MiraLAX and Dulcolax. I decided that I would prefer this method over drinking this nasty stuff that I was prescribed. The mere volume of liquid that I would be expected to consume was more than my body could handle. Having been unable to eat solid foods for six weeks I knew that there should be little waste in my intestines.

CHAPTER 6: DISCOVERY

Parasites

November 19, 2019, the day prior to my colonoscopy, I had gone to the bathroom at work. I had the usual abdominal pains that I had grown accustomed to. When I began to wipe, I immediately noticed that there was no fecal matter on the toilet paper. It sure felt like I had passed stool. Startled, I stood up and looked in the toilet.

What I saw was the most horrific image that I had ever thought possible. Staring into the bowl it looked like a bunch of intertwined hay, absent of any fecal matter. The color was off white and there had to be a hundred worms. They were not moving but I was instantly panicked. I quickly flushed the toilet so it is possible that they could have been alive. I pulled up my pants washed my hands and took off out of the bathroom. This was my new nightmare!

Feeling petrified, I swiftly went by my desk, grabbed my phone, and headed straight to the parking lot. I quickly called the nurse at my GIs office and proceeded to tell her what had just transpired. I said, "I do not know how to say this, so I am just going to say it. " She said, "okay." I then began to explain that I just passed a pile of worms with no fecal matter. She did not seem alarmed, and her response was very calm. She said, "that's ok, the doctor will see it in your colonoscopy tomorrow."

I was frantic and lost. I quickly texted my husband who responded that he didn't want to know and didn't want to hear about it. His response was clear that he was just as alarmed as I was. The word petrified was not even close to what was happening inside my soul. I had no idea what was in store for me at this point, but all of this was starting to make sense.

The following day, November 20, 2019, my daughter took me to my scheduled colonoscopy. My husband was still out of state, and I had to have someone there for me for this surgical procedure.

We arrived for my appointment and sat in the lounge as I completed the paperwork awaiting my turn. The form they had me complete specifically stated that I should not make any important decisions or drive for 24 hours.

It was my time to be called back to the pre-op room to get ready for my procedure. The nurses were awesome, efficient and wasted no time. I waited a brief time before I was taken to the procedure room where I was put under anesthesia.

I was awakened back in the recovery room by my daughter, jokingly telling me she had a will for me to sign. We both laughed as it was a very funny statement.

Shortly after, the doctor came to advise me that the only thing he found was a few diverse polyps but no parasites. He removed the polyps and sent them out for testing. I was not aware that the doctor only requested testing for cancer and H. Pylori which both returned negative.

My daughter and I left the office and went out for breakfast. It was nice to visit even though I was full of fear. Because of our busy work schedules, we didn't get to see each other a lot. Life was busy for everyone and especially for my daughter raising her children. After we ate our breakfast, we went home.

My mind was set with worry and confusion on my drive back home and I didn't want to talk to anyone. I was puzzled and needed to make sense of all that had transpired over the previous year. I had the feeling of being in a race all hyped up in a hurry to go nowhere, trying to find answers.

By this point I noticed that I was starting to get, what I call, "pimple blisters" which were very painful and would not heal. Initially, they appeared as a pimple, then formed into a blister leaving a hole in my skin. I had one behind my left ear, my left back shoulder blade, my right ankle, and right shoulder. I also had a stiff neck on my left side, which had affected me for months.

The pain in my entire body now made sense to me. I now knew, that I was being eaten alive. The nodule and cysts in my feet; the pimple blisters, and the massive amount of pain that I had experienced, not to mention my loss of organs were all due to these parasites. How did all of these doctors miss this?

As I began to ponder the past events, I wondered if my inability to excrete and empty my colon was the reason for me having this parasite issue. The toxic stools that had filled my entire colon with no way to evacuate the waste had exacerbated my condition. I had complained about my inability to relieve myself since my appendectomy, but my concerns and my condition were being ignored.

My teeth breaking showed me that I was severely nutrient deficient as parasites will rob you of valuable nutrients. The weakness and exhaustion that I experienced was due to my malnutrition. In addition to this I had elevated bacteria levels caused by my parasitic infection and the toxic waste that they expel. My toxic waste was unable to be cleared from my body, and had compounded the bacteria levels in my body that, in turn affected my ears, head, and lungs. It became clear to me that I was completely infested with parasites. It was time to find help and quick!

I was back at work the following day on Thursday November 21, 2019. Worry filled my soul and fear had taken over my thoughts, not knowing where to find help. I had to use the bathroom and it happened again! I passed a second pile of worms identical to my first pile. It was the same measurement of that of a teacup saucer, again with no stool. There were at least a hundred. They appeared to be around 5 inches in length each.

Frantic, I again called Dr. Colon's office and asked for the nurse, who was not available, so I spoke to the lady who answered the phone. I expressed to her that I had a lot of pain in my abdomen and informed her that I had passed another pile of worms and demanded to be seen once again. She scheduled for me to return to the office the following day, November 22, 2019.

I arrived at the office and got checked in and waited about 5 minutes before they called me back. The nursing assistant came into the room and began taking my blood pressure and confirming the reason for my visit. I informed her that I had passed two piles of parasites with no stool. I remember her asking me if my parents had any mental illness disease. I answered, "no but what does that have to do with parasites? Even if my parents were mentallychallenged, it wouldn't negate the fact that I just shit two piles of worms!"

After she completed her tasks, Dr. Colon arrived. I told him that my pain all made sense to me now as well as the dysentery of my abdomen. I was being eaten alive. I informed him that I had passed two piles of worms and that I desperately needed his help. Interestingly, his physical response and gestures, would be practiced by all of my doctors who heard the word parasite.

"No that doesn't happen here, maybe in a a 3rd world developing country, but not here, Dr. Colon immediately responded, crossing his arms. "I think you have a hernia, so I am going to order a CT scan and find out." I said: "Doc, did you hear what I just said? I passed two piles of worms. I am being eaten alive." He said, "let us check you for a hernia first."

At no point did he examine my abdomen aside from looking at it. He didn't come near me, and he didn't touch my stomach. It was obvious that he was not hearing me. I would later learn that most doctors have a black box recording device in their exam rooms. I would love for all of my doctors to release copies of these recordings. Dr. Colon denied the possibilities of human parasitic infections occurring in the US. He did not document his comments in my records.

I took the order for the CT scan and left the office very frustrated and scared. I returned to work trying to produce a plan. I decided that I would go to the hospital in Chesapeake after work to get the CT scan and then proceed to the ER. The results of the of scan came back negative for hernias.

After leaving the radiology department at the hospital, I decided to go to the emergency room. I told the gray-haired doctor that I had passed worms and that I needed assistance. I really believed that I would receive help. The ER attending physician crossed his arms and said that there was little he could do without a stool sample. Knowing that I could not void my colon, I requested that the physician give me some medicine that would quickly allow me to excrete my bowels. He informed me that he could not accommodate me in this regard.

His behavior reminded me of the way Dr. Colon acted when I first told him I had parasites. He stood there with his arms crossed, leaning back in a defensive posture. It was my perception that, the reaction displayed from both the ER doctor and Dr. Colon was that of some sort of fear .

My stomach looked like I was nine months pregnant. The level of pain that I was experiencing I can only compare to the discomfort of food poisoning or having a baby. He

wouldn't help me regardless of my pleas for help. I removed the IV from my arm and left.

Another interesting fact was that the attending physician at the ER failed to note that the reason for my visit was parasites. My discovery of this fact would not come for another few months when I obtained copies of my medical records from this hospital.

Upon arriving back home, almost hysterical at this point, I stood in my dining room emotionally maxed out. I felt hopeless, lost, and alone thinking that I was the only person in the world with parasites. I didn't know where to go or how to find help.

In the corner of my eye, I noticed my dog's medicine on the hutch. I quickly retrieved it and typed the words "metronidazole and parasites" into the search engine. I learned that it was used primarily for parasites, and I made the decision that I was going to take one.

I immediately sent a text to my husband to let him know what I was taking in case I had some adverse reactions. At this point, I didn't feel like I had a choice as help was not coming from the doctors that I had seen.

After 3 days of taking this medicine, I could visibly see tiny worms just under my skin. Since my distension was only in my stomach not in my lower abdomen, it confirmed that my small intestine was loaded with parasites. The parasites were being affected by the dog medicine that I had taken. According to my research, the small intestines is the primary location of intestinal parasites which clearly explains why NO GI would do a capsule endoscopy on me after my numerous requests.

Dr. Beard

I had no idea what I was going to do, and I knew that I had to do something instead of sitting and crying. I had cried continuously due to the pain all over my body. My disappointment in the treatment that I had just received regarding my experience with the medical industry, began to fill my entire being with anger. When I was pissed and when I got angry enough, I could move mountains.

When I wasn't working, I spent my time on my porch searching for an infectious disease doctor to help me. My sister Lori also had spent time contacting numerous infectious disease firms to get me an appointment, but no one would take me without a positive identification indicating which parasite I had. While scrolling through my Facebook I came across a post from Dr. Beard. That was it! Dr. Beard! Now I just had to work up the courage to send him a text on this topic. I was embarrassed and wondered if I was the only one in this country suffering from parasites. This embarrassment would only last for a week before my rage and determination kicked into overdrive.

After realizing that my life counted on it, on November 26, 2019, I had the courage to reach out to Dr. Beard. I was ashamed and fearful that he would reject my claim of having parasites. I sent him a message with pictures to provide him with a visual of what was going on. He arranged to see me at his office the following day.

I got up the next morning, showered, and dressed to begin my

5.5-hour drive. I didn't care how far I had to drive to get the help I needed. I was always scared of driving long distances alone and did not do this often. The fear that I'd always had, seemed to evaporate, only to be replaced by my will to survive.

I blasted the radio for the duration of my drive, excited at the thought of getting help. Traffic around the Raleigh area was causing congestion, reducing my speed to around 20 miles per hour. I was frantic that I wasn't going to make it before noon when the staff went to lunch. When I knew that I would not arrive on time, I called the office to inform them that I would arrive during their lunch break. I was directed to come in regardless of the time of my arrival that they were waiting on me. THIS is why I love this man and his team! They ALWAYS put their sick patients before themselves. They are the most UNSELFISH group of people that I have ever had care for my family. If only we could clone them all and populate the world with wonderful people like them.

Once I arrived, I was escorted to a room for an immediate examination, where they listened to all that I said.

Emotional, I began to cry, and was comforted by their love and compassion for me and my feelings. The NP who was working under this doctor was also present in the room and began to examine the vials of worms that I brought with me. She thought it was really cool, which was entirely unlike how I felt. I begged her to continue her studies so that she could help people in the future.

Dr. Beard opened his computer and started looking up the different parasite pictures to help me identify my parasites. This was difficult to decipher for both of us. There were so many worms and they all looked like what I had in my stool. When I saw the worms in my stool, it was only for a few seconds even though the image is still ingrained in my mind. I was at a loss as to which parasite I had, however I picked the one that I felt matched what I saw. Ironically enough, I picked Taenia which is a tapeworm. Remember this reference in the future when I later discover that indeed, I had tapeworms.

Dr. Beard prescribed me Praziquantel to take for four weeks. He had advised me not to take them until I arrived home because I would need the bathroom. After I left his office, I headed to the CVS to pick-up my medicine only to discover that they didn't accept my insurance. The pills cost $468.00 US dollars for two pills. Because they didn't take my insurance the clerk gave me a discount by using an RX discount card, reducing my total to $211.00 US. I was given my medicine, left the pharmacy, got in my car, and drove to a gas station. I debated in my own mind whether to wait to take this medicine. I entered the store and bought a few waters along with something to eat so I could take the pills. I filled up my gas tank, opened the pill bottle and down the hatch they went. I couldn't wait! If I needed the restroom, I'd exit the highway and find a place to stop.

Within 2 hours of taking this medicine, most of the pain in my stomach was gone and the movement of the worms in my mouth had ceased. I was so happy on my return drive that I sang most of the way home astonished that the medicine had worked.

Wondering if I had gotten my parasites from one of my 5 dogs, I decided to get them examined. On November 30th, 2019, I had taken my two little dogs to the vet to have them checked and they were both fine. I then took my three large dogs to get tested for parasites and Daisy resulted with heart worms. We began her treatments, which would prove to be even more intense than what I would ever receive. This confirmed that we had active vectors in Pasquotank County.

I knew that vets were not allowed to examine human stools, still held some embarrassment, and didn't want to ask her to look at my pictures. When I got home, I sent a message to the clerk at my vet clinic to ask if they would look at a particular picture that I had taken of my stool. Their response was that, according to their best educated guess, it appeared to be a round worm.

I found it interesting that up to this point, that Dr. Beard's office was the only one willing to look at my parasites.

Another interesting fact is that the mainstream labs cannot look at a worm and identify it even with bench aids.

A veterinarian is highly trained to quickly identify parasites for our family pets. This now made sense to me. Vets are not permitted to examine and test human stool samples because, if they did, all who suffer would quickly get accurate answers regarding parasite identification.

I immediately sent a message to Dr. Beard and informed him of the vet's opinion and asked if these meds would treat round worms and his response was "no." He called in another prescription for 4 weeks of Albendazole. After I completed the 4 weeks of Albendazole therapy, I took the Praziquantel that I still had on hand. I wanted to make sure these bastards were gone.

Since I discovered that my problem was parasites, I felt that the issue in my toe was parasitic related. I decided to attempt once again to dig into the pinhole on my toe.

I put my foot in some Epsom salt to soak and soften the skin to work my way into this hole. I grabbed the toenail clippers and sanitized them, then I began to cut the tissue away surrounding the hole that had been present for the last several years. It was intriguing that it had never healed or closed.

The pain associated with digging into my tissue was incredible but it had to be done. I would soak my foot when the pain was too intense, as I worked my way down inside the tissue. When I got deep enough, I noticed something

white inside this pinhole. I grabbed the needle and began to squeeze my toe as I pulled this thing out. After several attempts, I finally pulled out what I would describe as something in comparable size and color of a grain of rice.

Dr. PCP2

I needed a new PCP because, Dr. PCP had released me from his practice for the comments that I made previously. I would have loved to keep Dr. Beard, but the distance was still a problem.

I was passing worms at an alarming rate with the Albendazole and Praziquantel and couldn't believe how many I had passed. Literally thousands had been expelled.

December 3rd, I found another local PCP to help me with my dilemma. I called the office, found out that they were accepting new patients, and informed them of my situation. Their first available opening was a few weeks out and I took it. Shortly after I made my appointment, a staff member called me back informing me that Dr. PCP2 wanted to see me the following day, December 4th, 2019.

My first visit with him was great, I cried, and he listened. I told him that my GI doctor didn't believe me, and Dr. PCP2, looked at me and said, "I believe you." I was elated. He said, "I will walk you every step of the way to the end" and I took him at his word. He stated that my liver and spleen were both enlarged. Previously, no doctor had mentioned this, but at least he knew what he was looking at.

I showed him where the parasites were in my stomach just under my flesh. We agreed to biopsy 3 of them and send them for testing. As he was taking them from my flesh, he said that he got 3 great specimens. I asked him if they were obvious specimens and he said yes, they were very good. I was so happy with Dr. PCP2 because we were going to find out precisely which parasites I had, to ensure that I was completely monitored to the end. He had his nurse draw my blood to run my labs. Now we just wait for answers. Looking back, I wish that I would have taken pictures, but at that time, I didn't yet have the courage to observe his removal of my specimens.

On December 5, 2019, my right shoulder became enlarged. I had a hard and painful knot appear at the base of my neck on my shoulder causing it to have the feeling of exhaustion.

I asked my son to rub my shoulder while he was in the kitchen cooking. He stated that he thought I needed to see a chiropractor. He said that my spine looked like it was out of place. I hadn't noticed this before but started to pay attention. Surprisingly, When I did learn to read my scans, I saw that there is a 90-degree angle on the imaging at the top of my spine that had a measurement noted on it. This tells me that someone saw this, however they chose not to disclose it. It was obvious that inflammation was causing the protrusion as though I had hunchback disease. The doctors never mentioned this to me. Thankfully, they did however record the measurement on my CT scan which is how I became aware of it and was able to make comparisons.

Dr. PCP2 sent a text message that my labs came back negative. I did not believe that this was even possible, because of the number of worms that I sent off in my stool sample. I was getting pissed because every test that I had thus far, came back negative. Even still, he was going to try to get me into an infectious disease dept at a notable university in NC. He really tried to get me the proper help from the experts, but we continued to hit a brick wall. The large university reviewed my scans and informed my doc that they didn't see anything at all, this included no swelling of my liver. This was strikingly similar to when Dr. Beard previously attempted to get me into another NC university. Again all our our attempts were failing.

After Dr. PCP2 received the feedback from the university, he concluded that there was nothing wrong with me discounting the size of my stomach and pain. This dance with American medicine continued for many months.

I was so irritated, that I decided to call the lab and requested that they not discard my specimen. I then requested to speak to the director of the lab. When Mrs. Director picked up the phone, I began to question her about their methods of testing. I was not in a mood to be friendly or polite as hard as I had tried. I would call her again later and cuss her out to no end. I was done with the corruption and lies of the medical industry and I let it be known.

In our conversation she advised me that they do not remove parasites for identification purposes. I went off! How in the hell do you not remove a worm to identify the species in an ova & para test? Isn't that why we call it ova & para? If we are going through an identification process of the parasite, it is imperative to slap that baby on a microscope slide and identify it. Nope! That is not what they do!

Foot Break

D ecember 2019, I was still taking the Albendazole and gained a huge relief from it as I continued to pass hundreds of worms every day. I stopped handling any food when I learned of my condition. I washed bedsheets and cleaned the entire house, including washing my sofas daily to keep my family safe.

One Saturday, my husband and son were visiting at a friend's house, helping him with some things. I drove by to see them and brought them some food. I had gotten out to my car and accidently dropped something on my foot. With the amount of pain I felt, I knew that I had broken a bone. I left the house and headed to Norfolk General to seek help. I waited for at least 30 minutes before I was seen. A nurse inserted an IV and then I was led back to a waiting area to continue to wait for my bed, until I was taken back to the exam room. One doctor entered the room and I advised him that I had a broken foot and additionally informing him that I had parasites. He left the room and returned with two additional men who I assume were doctors. They began rapid fire questions with their arms crossed about my knowledge of parasites. At that point, they asked for proof, and I showed them some pictures of my worms. They left the room and never did return. There was no x-ray on my foot or stomach being ordered. I waited for what seemed to be an hour before I removed my IV, put it in the biohazard waste receptacle and left.

What I was quickly learning was that the mention of the word parasites caused all of the doctors to behave differently. There was something bigger going on, and I was going to find out exactly what it was. In May 2021, when I was looking at the app for my medical history and labs on my phone, I noticed that this visit is absent from my records. Why would this visit have been left out of my medical records? Was it because I had mentioned that I had parasites?

With the Christmas holiday approaching, we decided that we were ready for a change of scenery and headed to Florida. I really wanted to have time to think and analyze everything that I was finding in my research. The boys wanted to go fishing and I wanted to sit and try to comprehend what had just happened to me.

We reserved a hotel in St. Petersburg that had a little balcony and beach front view. We made our way down and unloaded our things into the room and then ordered some pizza. As we ate, we discussed our plans for the day after we took a nap.

After we woke up, with fishing gear in hand, we headed to the beach to try beach fishing. I began to walk the beach looking for seashells while the boys were fishing. The waves were rolling in a little strong, impeding their hopes of catching any fish.

As I walked the beach I did so with care for my injured foot. It was still swollen and tender. Later that evening we went to the Skyway Fishing pier to do some night fishing. I didn't fish and really had just come along for the ride.

As the boys fished, I walked and listened to the water crashing against the piers, making occasional visits to our car. On my last trip to the car, I began to experience another attack. I didn't want to cut short the fun they were having, and tried to calm myself down. I felt as though I needed to leave and return to the hotel as if returning would somehow make my anxiety stop. The illogical thinking in the middle of a panic attack is unexplainable and made no sense to me or my husband. He had learned how to help me by this point. When I was having a panic attack, he would try to calm me down and assure me that I wasn't going to die. While I wanted to believe his words, it was difficult for me to do so. The boys packed up their fishing gear and took me back to the hotel.

I felt so bad that I ruined their fun. My illnesses had taken a large toll on my family and their happiness because they had to watch me suffer and were unable to help. Knowing I was bringing them grief added more stress to my heart. We were all suffering. I decided that it was best if I stayed back when they had their outings. I would limit my interference with their ability to have fun.

Spending time alone allowed me time to gather my emotions and get myself ready to fight against these parasites. This permitted me more time to dedicate to researching and learning about parasites and how to kill them. It had been more than a month since my discovery and time was of the essence. I had already lost 4 organs and was finding no help. There was no precise way for me to determine where they were located in my body or just how many parasites were left.

Dr. PCP2 and I had communicated several times by the medical text app when he advised me that my stool sample had come back negative. I questioned how the testing could have come back negative with so many worms in it. As we sent messages back and forth, he said that he wanted to see me on December 30, 2019. It wasn't so much what he said, but how it was said, that caused me to become concerned. I told my husband about the message, explaining that I had the distinct feeling that the doctor would try to say that I was crazy. My husband felt like I was misunderstanding the message but would accompany me on my visit.

It was Christmas day and we had stopped by the IHOP for breakfast. They talked about their next fishing trip to Treasure Island. I knew that I was going back to the hotel to have my alone time. I didn't mind being safely tucked away in the room and preferred being alone. After our meal they dropped me off and headed out.

I noticed that the medicine I was taking seemed to help me excrete a little more than I had been able to in the past year. I had used the bathroom several times and noticed things floating on top the water in the toilet. They looked like some sort of transparent eggs. I examined them to the best of my ability, while they were floating on top of the toilet water and could see a worm inside. I had never seen anything this unusual before in my life. I snapped some pictures and tried to examine them before taking the specimens out. I removed them from the toilet, depositing them in an empty Styrofoam cup, placing a plastic over it, then the lid. My plan was to add my newly collected parasite eggs by inserting them into my next stool sample specimen.

After a few hours alone I decided that I would walk to Treasure Island and meet them. I could use the exercise to get my blood moving as well as just enjoy the scenery of Florida. As I began to walk, I realized it was much further than I had imagined.

After I walked a mile or so, I decided that I would let the boys know that I was walking toward them. I wanted to make sure they knew where I was, but also was hoping they would pick me up. My husband responded and said they were on their way back and would pick me up. I had stopped at a bus stop in front of a large church to wait for their arrival, which was in just a few minutes.

I came to realize how much strength that I had lost when I had difficulty making it past a mile. In my mind, I thought that I could achieve this, but my body was screaming no! I was glad that I still believed in myself, even if my body couldn't perform.

I experienced the emotions of anger and fear. I needed an expert in parasitology and finding one was proving to be impossible. I emailed many parasitologists around the world and couldn't get a response.

According to the many studies that I read, all of the diseases that caused me to lose organs, were related to parasitic infections. If I was finding these studies and investing time to read them, how did the doctors not know about them?

Two things that I learned from reading the studies is that steroids and anesthesia were both dangerous catalysts. In many other countries prior to surgery patients are tested for parasites. The reason for the testing is that anesthesia causes the parasites to migrate to other areas, causing the body more harm. Was this perhaps why I had progressively gotten worse after taking the prescribed prednisone back in July 2018?

Was our dirt somehow better than anywhere else? Were our vectors, like mosquitoes, somehow not infective agents? Are the

Dengue infected mosquitoes being released by the EPA somehow at play here causing more carnage than need be? These are just a couple of the hundreds of questions that swirled around in my mind.

So, I started to study each of my medical issues, finding that parasites are very much related to all. There are numerous studies available stating these connections. So how is it that our doctors are not aware of this?

Several studies indicated that when a biopsy is performed on cysts, that they are taking part of the parasite in the extraction. They also stated that many parasites have the cancer genes in their body, naturally causing the biopsy to come back positive for cancer. This study only increased the number of questions I had. This article has since been archived.

I was quite disturbed when I stumbled on another study that stated, "1 in 3 Americans had undiagnosed parasites." published in 2014 and was archived in 2020. Doing this calculation means that 130 million Americans have parasites. But how was this possible? I was baffled how a person like me who eats little meat could contract parasites.

We know there is no surveillance on parasites with some small exceptions like Malaria or Babesia. Why not surveil others like helminths, filariasis, cysticercosis or echinococcosis?

You Need A Psychologist

We left Florida 4 days after Christmas and started our 14-hour trip back home. I had my specimens in a covered cup in hopes they could be utilized to determine what species I had inside me. After our arrival we unloaded our things into the house. I set the cup of what I believed to be eggs next to the porch outside. I didn't want to bring them inside the house to cause further issues for those that I loved. The next morning, I went to retrieve them only to find gnats all over the cup and inside. I was upset that I had let this happen without realizing what it meant. This taught me that my specimens had been living things at one point.

I continued to rehearse all that I had gone through trying to make sense of it all. I remembered that even while I laid in bed at night, gnats would be flying all around me. I had started a journal to keep track of my many symptoms, so I didn't forget and so my children would know how hard I fought, in case I died.

On December 30, 2019, my husband and I went to Dr. PCP2's office. I was nervous about what he would say but glad my husband was next to me. I had planned to be civil but when pushed against a wall, I know I am not. I had to focus and maintain my composure.

We were taken back to the room where my husband sat next to me. The doctor sat across the room with his back to the wall which was an unusual stance for a physician. I did notice this, but didn't think any more of it. He began talking about the results all coming back negative and that they had found nothing wrong with me. He explained that he made a mistake telling me that my liver and spleen were swollen, because the university saw nothing. He then went on and stated that he felt that I needed to see a psychologist! My husband quickly spoke up and stated that I was not crazy in an assertive tone. Dr. PCP2 then said he wasn't trying to say that I was, but all the testing had come back negative for parasites. It was in no doubt implied in what he was saying!

Looking back, to this point in time, Dr. PCP2 had already received my records from Dr. Colon. I had not yet learned that my family medical history had been changed, falsely indicating mental illness in my family medical history. Reflecting back, I can only assume, that when Dr. PCP2 saw those remarks that he concluded that I was mental too! The tension in the room had increased and I am sure we all felt uncomfortable, but at least we were learning how bias the medical profession was when it came to parasites.

Many doctors and hospitals were all saying that nothing was wrong with me, all the while taking my organs. My stomach was so large and hard I could barely bend over. Getting my shoes on became a chore and picking something up from the floor was impossible. I was losing sensations to urinate, which I thought was renal failure. I no longer had to run to the bathroom after waking up in the morning and could go hours more without urinating.

What I will learn later after sifting through my thousands of medical records from the past year is that it was noted from the radiology department at the hospital in Chesapeake that my liver was swollen. They saw it and noted it in my file but never told me. My liver was measured at 17.76cm on January 19, 2019. According to the CDC it should measure around 7-8cm for a woman and mine was more than double that size. My CBD (common bile duct) measured at .81cm (8.1mm) and according to the CDC the normal range is 1.8 to 5.9mm. Again, not one doctor investigated this, nor was I informed.

When we got back home, I headed to the porch to sit and cry. I had to figure a way to get further treatment and be monitored by an expert. But how?

About a week later I became aware of some changes in my mouth. I had already taken both Praziquantel and Albendazole but now my tongue had white and green stuff on it. A lesion had appeared just under my left tonsil but there was no pain associated with it. There were visible lines on the inside of my cheek. The lines looked as though there was a worm just under the tissue. It measured about eight inches long and the length went from one cheek through my lip to the other cheek. I had no pain with exception of a swollen lip that would randomly appear where the black dot is under my lip.

While I was disappointed with Dr. PCP2, I did return to see him for the white and green stuff on my tongue called thrush. This is also known as candida albicans, commonly referred to as a yeast infection.

He prescribed Nystatin, a liquid medicine, for me to take. After taking it for three days, I became symptomatic. My throat started hurting, my lesion became achy, and the gland on my left side of my neck became enlarged. I began to panic and drove around town near the doctor's office debating whether or not I should call the office. After I pulled into a parking lot, I called the office to advise them of my symptoms. I was directed to come to the office where I was taken to the exam room.

Shortly after the doc came in, he heard my concerns then began to examine my mouth. After my examination he stated that he didn't see anything. He didn't see thrush, he didn't see a lesion, he saw nothing! How in hell did he not see anything, yet he had prescribed Nystatin just days before? This whole thing was getting more bazaar each day. I left the office pissed, so much so, that when I got home, I sent a message to his office and fired this guy. There are many who continue to face the battle of parasites, understanding the emotional trauma and gaslighting that takes place in the medical arena. I have fielded many conversations with hundreds of people across the world who have shared the same experience.

Knowing that the CT scans held the key to many of my issues, I continued to learn to how to read CT scans. I had over 40 scans done in about a year and knew that something was being overlooked. This may have been either purposely or accidently, however I believed it was   the first of the two possibilities. I began to study anything that I could find on the internet and watched lots of videos. I joined many radiology groups and followed along with their teachings. I would find out what they were missing!

Neurologist

J an 17, 2020
I wasn't having much luck getting into any infectious disease universities by referrals, so it was going to be up to me to take charge of my health and my medical issues. I was on my own at this point. I started to call every infectious disease facility that I could find on the east coast, from New York to Florida. Without any luck I decided to see the neurologist that was referred several months prior who was 5.5 hours away.

I called and scheduled my appointment for January 17, 2020, hoping this would be the breakthrough that I needed. I didn't know at this point, that doctors received little to no education or training about parasites.

Radiologists were not taught how to read them in scans; doctors weren't taught how to recognize their related symptoms and we have no surveillance systems in place. We also do not do any studies on American citizens because, we were all conditioned to believe that parasitic infestations do not happen here.

I drove the 5.5 hours to see Dr.Neuro, having adequate time to prepare for what I would say to him. I was unsure whether or not I should even mention parasites, since this word seemed to be taboo. Once I arrived, I was weighed and taken back to the exam room where the doctor wasted no time coming into the room. The staff were courteous, efficient, timely and really seemed to respect my time.

This office is part of a large medical group enabling doctors to see all my records and scan results. I told the doctor about my past diagnoses and my brain lesion. He seemed like a nice guy and was receptive of what I was saying, so I decided that I would tell him that I had parasites. I opened the pictures on my phone and asked if he wanted to see them. He was very much interested to see them and took my phone to browse my pictures. His attention to the pictures said it all for me, he did believe that I had an issue with parasites.

I informed Dr. Neuro that I had been experiencing constant migraine headaches which made me feel unbalanced and clumsy. He explained to me that he had little knowledge of parasites and felt that I needed to see an infectious disease doctor. I told him of the troubles I had trying to get in to see a specialist. His reply was that I did not need to worry because there was an infectious disease (ID) doctor right next door and that he would talk to him. I was about to jump out of my skin with excitement as I was hopeful that this was where I would get help.

Infectious Disease

H arrisonburg VA Feb 13, 2020
Within a few days, I received a call from the office of the infectious disease doctor, to schedule an appointment. I was super excited believing that I would finally see an expert. My appointment was made for February 13, where I would once again make the 5 ½ hour trip.

At this point, I thought that all infectious disease doctors knew about parasites. It would take more time to discover that my assumption was wrong.

On the day of my appointment, I left home early to ensure that I arrived on time. Once I arrived, I checked in and was taken back to the exam room. After the nurse took my vitals, the doctor entered the room and sat down.

Dr. ID seemed nice enough and didn't gaslight me like the others had. He asked me what was going on and requested to see some of the pictures that the neurologist had spoken about. I opened my phone with obvious excitement and handed it over to him. I went on to explain that a vet had identified one, as a round worm.

He showed little emotion as he studied my pictures and said he was unable to identify any of the parasites. He did not order any labs to be drawn but wanted me to submit to 3 more stool sample tests. I asked him some questions surrounding the stool tests to see what his knowledge base was, and found out that he had no idea of the processes that are followed.

I had already done 4-5 stool sample submissions at this point that all came back negative. There was no way that these tests should have come back negative for the sheer number of worms that were sent in. I didn't think another test would be beneficial because it was the same lab that would perform the studies. Why waste my time and money on failed testing procedures? That was the end of this guy!

When I spoke to the director of a nationwide lab, I was informed that they DO NOT extract the worms from the stools for identification purposes. Additionally, she advised me that they only look for eggs. Next she alerted me to the fact that there had to be a very specific number of eggs present. She divulged to me that they were only required a mere 10 minutes per stool study. I questioned her on the educational level of those who were doing the studies. She then informed me that they receive 3 days of training spending a total of eight-hours each day.

Sedimentation studies take a minimum of 25 minutes and 5 seconds just in the prepping for the test. So, then the question becomes, are they even performing this test? Or are they only doing a smear test? But even if it were a smear test, it would take more than ten minutes.

The next issue is the shipping time involved prior to the examination. Examination of the stool must be done without any delay according to the CDC. For stool that contains trophozoites and cysts, the examination must take place within 30 minutes of the patient passing it. Cysts must be examined within 1 hour of excretion. The longest amount of time from excretion to examination is 1 day, and that is ONLY if the stool has been preserved and refrigerated. The more time that passes, a greater number of parasitic eggs will die off. The eggs must be viable (live) to be counted for a positive test result. All worms should be removed from the stool then tested using the flotation, or sedimentation techniques.

So, if the stool must be examined within 30 minutes, and we are shipping the specimen to a central location, sometimes out of state, there is no way this adequate timing is being followed. So now we must ask if this is by design or ignorance? Why is the lab facility not testing right then and there? The parasitic eggs are continually dying and must be viable causing many false negatives!

The techs can do 1-3 smears on a 3x1 slide, but this does not allow them to see the entire sample meaning that they are not looking at the entire specimen that the patient submitted. The eggs could be in the stool that the patient didn't collect, or it is in the other half of the collection. So, the chances of getting a positive result is slim to none.

When we look at the words of the CDC guidance for examinations, they state that fecal examinations are both labor intensive and require a skilled microscopist. So, here is my thinking …. if the tech had not received formal education at great length in parasitology, to have the ability to quickly identify the eggs without using bench aids, no one will ever get diagnosed! Cashiers get more than 24 hours of training and here we are thinking that anyone can easily learn about parasites in 3 days? It goes without saying that this is virtually impossible.

According to the CDC, the best testing methods include the DFA (direct fluorescent assay), the EIA (enzyme immunoassay), and rapid dipstick testing. These tests are suggested because of the lack of experience in the labs for microscopy examination. I can tell you that I don't know any infectious disease doctor or physician of any kind, who had suggested any of these tests. Why was it that none of these tests were offered to me, if they did know about them?

Many doctors across this nation don't know the processes of parasite testing. They are simply relying on the labs to do the testing who will in turn advise them of the results. Doctors use these findings to treat their patients. When the result findings come back negative, doctors are quick to judge and diagnose a patient as having "delusional parasitosis."

This diagnosis, while I didn't receive it, is the biggest bunch of bullshit I have ever seen! It is the biggest lie in the medical industry. The craziest thing is that the doctors don't even know it! So, do we blame the doctors? Or the CDC for failing to hear the cries across this nation of those who suffer. Personally, I blame them all!

I think they all carry the responsibility of the failures as they leave many ill lives in their wake. With all of the knowledge that we have in the medical industry, how is this parasite issue so overlooked? This brings me to my next thought, how is it possible to think that Americans are exempt from contracting parasites? Is our dirt somehow better than the rest of the world? Is our recycled shit water somehow safer? Do the vectors somehow know not to transmit their parasites to an American citizen? These questions, as bazaar as they may sound, are not as ridiculous as you may think. The answers to them all is "YES"! We have been conditioned to believe that by some great miracle, all parasites have crossed the borders and LEFT this country!

I decided this doctor was not going to be the right guy to help me, and that I had to keep looking. As I continued my search, I came across another university in DC. I researched their infectious disease facility and completed the request for an appointment. They called me back on the following Thursday and scheduled me for March 16, 2020, at 8:30am.

University in DC

arch 2020, we headed to DC after work and found that there was little traffic, thanks to Covid. We arrived at the hotel and noticed on the drive through town that there were hardly any places open to eat.

After we checked-in, we asked the clerk if he was aware of any place to grab a bite to eat. We were then directed to a restaurant a few doors down. After we took our belongings to our room, we headed out to grab a bite to eat. There were few patrons in the restaurant as fear gripped the city. We were seated at what seemed to be, a great distance from the other patrons, which I preferred anyways. We ate our meal and headed back to our room where we quickly fell asleep.

The next morning, we got up and decided to walk to the office. We had trouble finding the building we were looking for and approached a guard at the hospital. He was at the door prohibiting people from entering until they got through the safety protocols. He had his temperature scanners ready to go, checking the foreheads of all individuals prior to entry.

I explained that I was trying to find the office of the infectious disease department but was a little displaced. I showed the guard the text message that I had received regarding my appointment. We were pointed in the direction of the building that we were looking for, just two blocks away.

Elated that we were so close, we hurried along. Upon entry of the facility, we were met with another security guard who then went through the Covid questions, scanned our foreheads, allowing us to enter. We proceeded to the 3rd floor, checked in and were seated in the waiting area.

While waiting, I had to cough! How was I going to cough without everyone looking at me like I have the plaque? I then noticed a water dispenser, and thought, I will get a glass of water and act like it went down the wrong tube and cough, so, I did!! It worked like a charm.

Only moments later we were taken back to the exam room. The doctor and an intern came in the room where I was met with respect and dignity. They did not look at me like I was crazy or a bother to them, but instead, they listened to what I said without saying a word. The young intern sifted through my medical charts as if she were a speed reader, however I knew that there was no way she was reading everything as written. I opened my phone and began to show them pictures of my worms and stools. The doctor had little to say, but suggested that I have 3 more stool tests. They ordered a parasite identification test, which I thought was different than the Ova & Para test. They gave me the orders and sent me down to the lab to pick up my supplies. I was under the impression that this lab was one of their own. I thought that they utilized state-of-the-art testing. Upon arrival I recognized the name of the lab and immediately knew that this was not going to work. I was upset that this same lab was associated with the university. I was extremely familiar with the protocols and procedures that they followed.

Disappointed in this discovery, my husband mentioned that there is a possibility that they do things differently because they were in the university. I knew in my heart of hearts that wasn't going to be the case, but I picked up my supplies to submit to the test. We went back to the hotel, packed up our belongings and headed back home. I felt like this was another wasted trip and wasted expenditure and it was!

I decided that I would do the tests and hope that my husband was right, that they would ship it to the university for testing. After I got my samples, I drove them to the local lab to drop off, only to discover they were sending them off to the very lab that had, on multiple occasions performed my previous tests.

In my research, I read that serology testing was the best method of testing and I requested an order for this test from the doctor. To my surprise my request was denied. The intern didn't feel that I needed this testing because my samples came back negative. Isn't that precisely why she should have ordered them? Isn't it their oath to help me and not hurt me? Why would they deny any test that would possibly give me the right answers? I was done with this place!

CHAPTER 7: DOCTORS

Urgent Care

I was still experiencing the same symptoms in my mouth from having taken the Nystatin and decided that I needed to get it checked out. I decided to go to the Urgent Care and have them look at it. I was checked in and taken to the exam room when the NP came in. She examined my mouth and remarked that it was some sort of stone and that she could "knock it off." Of course, I agreed to do this.

She retrieved a long wooden stick that looked similar to a chopstick. I opened my mouth, and she began attempting to remove it. I was experiencing gag-reflex, so she would stop on occasion providing me breaks, to lessen the potential of me throwing up.

After several failed attempts she went to retrieve another stick to depress my tongue down while she worked to remove the stone. Suddenly, she exclaimed, "oh my god... it looks like a worm." I knew I had worms, but hearing those words caused me to heave uncontrollably. At the time, I was not aware that she had removed it. The worm was on the end of the stick that was still in my mouth. The heaving caused her to drop it right down my throat.

At this point, I decided that it was safe enough to tell her that I had parasites. She responded that their office had seen and treated several people for parasites recently. I was not, however given anything for them. I was full of disappointment that I had caused her to lose the specimen that she removed. This could have been the one thing that I needed to help me get diagnosed and I screwed it up.

Regardless of whether it was a stone or a worm, it was now removed from my mouth, and I had to hope that I passed it. The lesion remained in my throat but no longer caused any pain. I still had the stiff neck on my left side making it difficult to turn my head to the left. I also had the swollen lymph node that Dr. PCP2 could not see.

A few weeks after I decided that I would go back to Urgent Care and have them look at my foot as it was still swollen and sore. I went in and saw the doctor who did X-rays. I found that I had two fractures, and that the pins from my prior bunionectomy had gone through my bone. With every step that I took, I experienced pain from the top to the bottom of my foot. The Urgent Care gave me a temporary boot and a referral to see an orthopedic physician.

Orthopedic

I called an orthopedic, Dr. E in E-City and was told to drop off my x-rays at their office located in the hospital. A couple of days had passed, and I didn't hear back from them. After calling the doctor's office I was informed that the doctor would not treat me because he "didn't go behind other doctors." He suggested that I return to the same doctor who put the pins in my foot some 20+ years prior.

I didn't even remember the name of the doctor who did my procedure, let alone know if he was still in practice or even alive. I couldn't remember his location to drive by, because it was 23 years ago. It was difficult for me to believe that this was the reason for the doctor not seeing me. Doctors routinely treat patients who have been treated by other doctors for a variety of reasons.

For everything that I had experienced within our medical industry, it amazed me that anyone could survive them. Was I in the wrong city or area of the country trying to get help? Or was our system broken beyond repair?

I continued to call around when I found another orthopedic practice in Norfolk and scheduled my appointment with them. After I arrived and got checked in, it was only minutes later when Dr. Ortho took me back to the exam room. He stated that he wanted to do another foot x-ray and he did. After the results were read, he returned to my room and stated that he only saw 1 fracture and didn't know what the previous radiologist was talking about in relation to the pins. He said that I needed to see their surgeon, who was in Virginia Beach. He gave me a different boot to wear until I saw the surgeon. I left the exam room and went to the check-out clerk who then scheduled my appointment for the surgeon.

I arrived at the appointment to see the surgeon on the specified date. Covid was still bringing fear to the nation. I wasn't acclimated to wearing a mask and didn't bring one in with me. As I entered the facility, I saw people everywhere in the foyer sitting next to each other. The doctor's office, located on the first floor only allowed one person in at a time and had everyone sitting next to each other in the hallway. This was ironic that they wanted people to stay away from each other, yet they are piled on top of each other.

I got to the desk without a mask, they took my temperature and into the elevator I went. When I arrived at the second floor, I was stopped from entering the surgeon's office because I didn't have a mask on. I turned around and went back to my car with the hope that I had a mask. After rummaging through the glove box and console I finally found one. With my mask in hand, I headed back to the medical building.

Upon my second entry, the desk clerks wanted to ask me where I was going before they did another temperature check. I had just gone through this checkpoint with the same personnel moments earlier, and now they wanted to ask a bunch of questions? I made it through the check point again and headed back upstairs.

Once upstairs, I went through another check point and was seated until I was taken back to the exam room. The doctor arrived only moments afterwards and I began to discuss the x-rays of my left foot. He asked how I broke my foot, opening the door for my explanation. I told him that I had parasites. I further explained, that my body was very weak from being robbed of nutrients by the parasites. I advised the doctor that because of all of this, my bones were fragile, being prone to fractures and breakage. I explained that the item that I dropped on my foot was only a couple of pounds. At this point his whole demeanor changed.

After making this statement about parasites the doctor then said he didn't see any fracture at all! This was interesting because even the orthopedic saw one fracture. Now this guy does not see anything. This is a prime example of what I have dealt with in the medical community for more than 2 years. No two doctors or radiologists can see or say the same things. It amazed me that as soon as that magical word "parasites" was spoken, all doctors lost their minds!

I began to think that there was a larger cover-up taking place and that it was bigger than just Dr. Surgeon having caused me injury. Whatever was going on was much larger, and it had a lot to do with those ruling the medical profession.

Dr. Expert

B efore finding Dr. Expert, I phoned nearly every infectious disease office on the east coast. I had seen 2 by this point and both were worthless. I called his office in early March 2020 and spoke to the receptionist. I explained that I had been passing parasites but found difficulty getting help from an infectious disease doctor who knew anything about them. She told me that this was a common statement from most patients who called. I asked if Dr. Expert knew about parasites, and she assured me the doctor did. Identification was not required because he had the expertise needed. There were no words to explain my excitement. My appointment wait was less than 2 weeks.

Filled with anticipation, I could hardly wait to leave the house that morning. I tried not to get too excited because my past experiences didn't necessarily indicate that I would find success. I got in my car and started my 3.5 hour drive. Once there, I was taken back to the exam room where the LPN checked my vitals prior to the grand entrance by the doctor.

Shortly afterwards, a nurse practitioner came into my room. I began to tell her about the events related to my passing of parasites and opened my phone to show her pictures of the parasites in my stools. She interrupted me stating, "I need to get the doctor." The two of them switched places and I began to share my story with Dr. Expert, showing him my pictures.

As I am going through the pictures, he is identifying them by name. "That's a tapeworm, that's a round worm" etc. I couldn't believe it. I finally found a doctor who was able to identify different parasites and knew what to do to help me. Two prior infectious disease doctors said, either that they didn't see anything, or that they didn't know what they were seeing. This was an incredible moment for me, and I knew I was finally at the right place!

The doctor asked me about the work that I had previously done over the years, as he tried to decipher how I may have contracted the parasites. At that time, I was an HR manager, and enlightened the doctor, as to the nature of my past professional roles. He asked if I had ever handled meat or produce. Of course I had, including the stocking of produce, culling many times , as well as cleaning meat bunkers. The doctor indicated to me, that in his professional opinion, my parasites may have been contracted during my previous employment activitties. Makes sense to me!

Dr. Expert went on to explain that he wanted to do more testing and told me not to get excited as blood and stool labs rarely resulted in positive identification of parasites. The person who needed to draw my labs was unavailable and would return following the day. At the time I did not realize that this doctor used the same lab that had failed me numerous times before.

My husband decided that he would drive me back to the doctor's office for my labs. Once we arrived, I was taken directly back to the phlebotomist. She drew about 12 vials of blood and gave me a specimen container for my stool sample. After the sample was collected, I would have to drive back to the office to deliver it.

Unable to void my colon, I had taken Dulcolax to get a sample of my stool for testing. We headed down the road again 3.5 hours to drop off my samples for testing to my doctor's office. It was important to get this done prior to my 2 weeks follow-up in hopes that we could get proof of what had invaded my body.

What I didn't know, but would learn later, was that laxatives, herbs, and many meds will cause the testing results to be inaccurate. Why have I never been informed that the medicine that I was taking to help me poop was preventing me from receiving an accurate analysis? This is a known fact, and we are not advised to avoid this particular list of medicines that are contraindicated to a successful analysis. Medicines that should be avoided for two weeks prior to testing are: laxatives, antibiotics, antiacids, Pepto-Bismol, antiparasitics. In the past 15 months, many doctors were acutely aware that I was not able to void my colon without taking these medicines. All of these doctors failed to investigate why.

I went back for my two-week follow-up to obtain my results. I was not at all surprised when I received the news that all of my tests were negative. My labs showed many abnormalities. My eosinophils (elements of white blood count that are known to fight parasitic infections) were higher than the doctor preferred. My sedimentation rate was exceedingly high, red blood cells enlarged, amongst many other things.

It was only because the doctor was able to identify my parasites, by my pictures, that he put me back on Praziquantel. My treatment continued periodically for 14 months. Therapy should not ever consist of a "one pill and you are done" approach. The sheer number of eggs that parasites can lay, can go upwards of 230,000 a day and they hatch every 12-14 weeks. It is imperative to get treatment for a minimum of 3 cycles. If cysts are present, the treatments can last for years, since cysts can remain viable for up to 10 years.

I left the office excited to start the proper therapy and stopped by Walmart on the way home to pick up my prescription to get started immediately. After a couple of days, I noticed that I had crawling sensations in my face. It appeared that this higher prescription dose was the impetus causing worm activity. The worms moving in my face were unbearable and too much for me to handle. The thought of suicide had entered my mind, but I knew I didn't have the courage to take my own life. The lack of courage would be my saving grace. Back in November when I had gone to see Dr. Beard, I was feeling parasites in my mouth. When I took my first dose of Praziquantel it all stopped. Now taking this higher dose of Praziquantel, I started to re-experience parasitic movement in my face.

The gratitude that I have for Dr. Expert is immense, and he will forever have my respect. He is an expert in his field and his heart is in the right place. Unlike the other doctors that I had, this doctor truly was the expert.

Charity Lee Armistead-Carroll

In my search for answers and understanding, I found and joined various different social media platforms related to parasites. I was amazed at the sheer number of people on the many sites who were suffering and begging for help. This is where I learned that I was not alone as I had previously thought.

This is how I came to know a young lady named Charity. We were both on this same platform and I was trying to encourage them all to come out of the shadows. We needed to band together, and be willing to publicly speak out regarding this unspoken epidemic that pervaded the United States.

I was quickly met with resistance from the leader of this particular group who questioned whether or not I was an undercover reporter. It was obvious to me that my stance was causing uneasiness amongst them. My goal was not to bring fear to these members, but instead to organize and expose all that we knew. I decided that my presence was bringing too much fear, so I left the group.

A month after I left the group, I received a message from Charity. We had never directly spoken and didn't know each other. In no time at all, we had become particularly good friends. She tried to explain to me why so many of the sufferers stayed in the shadows.

Many had fears of losing their children due to overzealous

doctors diagnosing "delusional parasitosis." Many women had already lost their children from doctors directly reporting to child protective services. Families have been torn apart from these inaccurate diagnoses. It is bad enough when parents are sick and fighting for their lives, but to destroy their families is unacceptable. They have been conditioned to think that parasites are not in our dirt, food or water? THIS is why I fight for change.

Charity opened my eyes to the surveillance of vectors, or the lack thereof, and the importance of getting this topic into the spotlight. She taught me how to use a microscope, bench-aids, and shared her advice with me. In no time at all, I got the hang of it, and was able to get clear pictures of my parasites.

Although we knew that I had tapeworms, we did not know exactly which tapeworms I had. To differentiate between the echinococcus or cysticercoses, we needed to examine the tails. Charity and I spent uncountable hours collaborating on different elements of parasitic infections.

Charity asked me to promise her, that when I got well, I would continue my fight to help the others who were afflicted with parasites. I am keeping my promise to both Charity and my kids. No change can come until we start the conversation with our elected officials. They need to hear our stories and understand how broken our system is in its entirety.

Charity grew up on a farm and shared her knowledge of parasites with me. Farmers are the most commonly afflicted with parasites in our society, followed by anyone who works in or around dirt.

She had numerous impressive pictures of her microscopic slides, revealing several types of worms that she is personally infected with. The attending health care professionals that examined her have completely ignored the evidence that she had shown them. She even has a video showing a worm swimming in the toilet after she urinated. When she took her live worm to her doctor, they wouldn't even look at it!

Amid all that was transpiring, I went back to see Dr. Surgeon in April 2020. My intent was to continue my conversation, conveying that (in my opinion) I felt that he had injured me. After I entered the office, I was taken back to the exam room. When the doctor came in, we began to talk. I expressed concern that he had caused me injury and directly inquired whether or not anyone other than himself had worked on me during my surgery. He told me that no one had.

I left the office with no answers. About a month later, I had left a message on the voicemail of his nurse. I asked her to have Dr. Surgeon go back and review my scans. It was my belief that whatever mistakes the doctor made were in the scan. The following week I received notification by mail that this doctor was indeed retiring and giving his 30-day notice.

After I received copies of my medical records in May 2020 from Dr. Colon's office, I shared them with Charity. In her wisdom and brillance, she quickly took notice of my family medical history pointing out that my GIs office had changed it. She stated that both of my parents were now documented in my medical reports as having been diagnosed with mental illness disease.

I instantly became livid and couldn't send an email fast enough to my doctor's office. This was nothing short of falsification of my records. I wanted to know the reason why this doctor would knowingly fabricate such a falsehood and go so far as to enter this erroneous information in my medical records.

The coordinator on the other end of the phone was unable to assist me, so she got the office manager involved. After many emails flew back and forth, the office manager called me. A screaming match between the two of us ensued and neither of us were budging from our positions. I wanted the false information removed and she wouldn't remove it.

There had never been any diagnosis of mental illness disease in our entire family, and that includes my cousins. This was the biggest lie ever told and I was shocked that any doctor would have done such a thing. I couldn't help but wonder if this was the reason that I had been unable to find help. I formally filed a complaint with the VA state medical board. After several months of investigation they found no wrongdoing by this doctor's office. I have the evidence that my records were changed over a two-day period. That is a fact, the doctor had no evidence that I had any family history of mental illness. How could there be no wrongdoing when the evidence was undeniably clear?

The only correction that the GI's office made was adding an addendum to the end of my medical file. Not appearing until the very end of my file and having such a small size of the print, deems this insertion highly unlikely to be read by any other doctor who is reviewing my file. Generally speaking, doctors don't go through the entire file and read every single word.

CHAPTER 8:
IDENTIFICATION

Dr. Robin Overstreet

O ne evening I sent an email to Dr. Overstreet, politely asking for his help in identifying which parasites I had. He immediately responded that he had helped other individuals and would try to help me. I was excited, yet at the same time worried, that something may scare him off.

Dr. Overstreet was an Emeritus Professor at The University of Southern Mississippi. He studied marine biology and parasitology, not just in the United States, but traveled the world. He is world renowned in his expertise of parasitology and has written over one hundred studies related to marine parasitology and pathology. I had to pray that this was the doctor who would help me distinguish which tapeworm I had. I was hoping that he would take the time to teach me as much about parasites as my brain would hold.

It was only a couple of days after sending my email that Dr. Overstreet called me. We spoke at great lengths about my situation. His education and knowledge made him a phenomenal mentor. I absorbed every bit of information possible. He freely shared his incredible wealth of scientific research regarding parasites.

We continued to talk frequently about various subjects, not just parasites. Dr. Overstreet would suggest different microscopic technique including; magnification strength, lens, and dye to use.

It was important to get the illumination of the parasites intestines as well as the tail. I tried multiple strengths and settings and used a smaller lens because I was using a higher magnification.   He taught me about different and specific elements of the tapeworm that I needed to capture under the microscope. This was necessary in order for me to determine exactly which tapeworm I had.

I continued to slap every worm on a slide to get this information. I worked hard to learn and practice the many techniques. I used my phone camera to video record and took pictures of the specimens as well. It was a matter of life and death to determine which tapeworm I had.

We spoke several times over a few weeks period and he offered to look at the parasites to identify them. I prepared a couple of specimens and mailed them overnight UPS. Unfortunately, by the time the package was received, the sample had deteriorated to such a degree that he was unable to identify the parasites. I learned that parasites should be placed in a proper preservative such as formalin.

I sent some of my scope pictures and my parasite was identified as cysticercosis. This was exactly what I had hoped for. I have such immense gratitude for this man, however I feel that, no words can express my sincere appreciation. He could have been like all the others who ignored my pleas for help, but his heart is just too big not to help. His generosity of time was more than I could have ever hoped for.

Our relationship has grown into a nice friendship where our conversations are no longer about parasites. It is so wonderful to have met a person who through his love of teaching was able to help me understand what I was seeing under the scope and dealing with in my life.

I am so lucky to have a friend like Dr. Overstreet!

Medical Records

I went to the hospital in Chesapeake to retrieve my medical records which ended up being more than 800 pages long. The reproduction cost for my 800 copies was $175.00 U.S. I needed to review my records to see what was being overlooked. With the massive size of my file, it became an impossible task. This sizable file represented just one of the three hospitals I had been to, not including several doctors that I had seen.

As I was going through these records, my mind was still stuck on the GI's office changing my family medical history. Why would the doctor put false information in my file? Why did the office never write down any of their own unprofessional comments? For instance, the remark made by the doctor when he folded his arms, stating to me that parasites don't happen in the US, but only in third world countries.

It was interesting that on the same day that I disclosed that I had parasites, my family medical history was changed without my knowledge. This was only two days after my initial visit.

My records from Dr. Colon's office, with the falsified family medical history changes had gone to several other doctors' offices prior to the addendum being added. Remember when I saw Dr. PCP2 who said I needed to see a shrink?

The PCP2 requested my records from Dr. Colon's office on

December 4, 2019. I didn't learn until May 2020 that my records had been falsified, so the records that were sent were not correct. It was after the doctor received my records from the GI with this false diagnosis, that he recommended that I see a shrink. The falsification of my family medical history, I believe, is what hindered my ability to be taken seriously, so that I could receive proper medical treatment.

When any doctor's office knowingly changes medical history or records of any kind, they hurt the patient in ways that cannot be measured. It is wrong on every level and should be considered a criminal act. These doctors should be held accountable for their negligence and intentional false assertions.

I also requested medical records from Dr. PCP's office back on November 29, 2019; and had no luck receiving them, so I filed a complaint with the VA. state medical board. I wouldn't receive my records until July 3, 2020. Under the HIPPA laws, doctors have 30 days to provide records after being requested. The investigator found no wrongdoing after all of my months of waiting.

As I continued to look through my medical records, I found many discrepancies. One hospital noted that I had complained about not getting my blood pressure medicine, when I had never been on any before. This was a trip to the ER where my blood pressure was 75/29. I was told to eat more salt, instead of the professionals getting to the cause of the massive fluctuations that I had experienced.

First Hernia

I continued to study, reviewing my scans in my computer when I saw a hernia. Prior to this, I had never had a hernia, so I didn't know what it felt like to have one, but my soul kept telling me that I did.

The doctors performed 22 scans on me from November 22,2019 to June 25, 2020. After 7 months and 22 scans, not one radiologist saw this? That was an average of 3 scans per months. It is important to ask why the medical professionals continue to scan me, rather than using my previous scans. Were my repeated scans to generate money, or were the professionals sincerely determined to find out what was wrong with me? I wanted to know why they had no concern about the impact of multiple scans on my liver and kidneys, with the constant use of contrast. But they didn't stop there, and I ended up having over 43 CT scans completed in a year and half.

I didn't go to school for radiology, however I spent a few months learning how to read scans. Am I an expert? Absolutely not, but I learned enough to see what the medical professionals all missed. I have about 43 scans to date that tell my story without having to say a word. I feel like I have an incarcerated hernia due to my symptoms and continued pain in my abdomen. The pain is nothing like that which was caused from my parasites, but a pain nonetheless.

A radiologist from Egypt who I had been following and learning from, agreed to accept and read my brain scan. I needed to know if it was parasitic or not. I didn't advise him that I had parasites so as not to impact his diagnosis. On July 5, 2020, I received a message from him. He didn't see a brain lesion, but instead, saw 3 calcified cysts. He asked me about my history with cysticercosis. I responded that we were trying to determine if my tapeworms were echinococcus or cysticercosis. He believed that I had cysticercosis.

I immediately thought that since I had his attention, I would ask about the scan showing my hernia. I instantly sent the image in question and told him that I thought I saw a hernia to which he replied, "yes hernia." I was so tickled with myself and my newly acquired skills. All of the time that I had invested in learning, was finally paying off. I requested that the radiologist give me a written report of his findings, but he informed me they were not allowed to draft reports for us in the US.

I sent my scans and pictures to another parasitologist in India who also confirmed that I had cysticercosis. Now that is 3 parasitologists and a radiologist/parasitologist from 3 different countries who have confirmed their findings for me, and they were all the same!

The following night on July 6th, I once again suffered enormous pain. It was around 11PM and I worried that my hernia was a life-threatening issue as the pain was almost unbearable. Being scared that this was the case, I went back to the E-City ER to have it checked.

The male nurse working on this night was the biggest asshole to date. As I was waiting in the exam room, I alerted him that I needed help. My pain was so intense that I thought I was dying. This nurse completely ignored me. His desk was only 5 feet away, so it wasn't like he couldn't hear me. I stood at the door trying to get him to help me, however he never once looked up. I suspected at this point that the hospital put a special "don't help this person" code in my chart. You know, the notes and remarks that the patient is not permitted to see.

I was not given anything for pain management and it didn't seem that there was a sense of urgency anywhere in the entire facility. It became clear to me that I was at their mercy.

It was sometime before they took me to get the CT scan of my abdomen. Once I arrived at radiology, I told the technician that I didn't want their doctors to read my scans and requested they be sent to another firm because they had misread every scan thus far. I told him a friend of mine, who was a radiologist confirmed that I had a hernia. I was informed that they couldn't send my scans to another facility because the radiology firm leased that space in the hospital. This is when I learned that the radiology departments in many hospitals are subcontracted space and that the hospitals don't own or operate them. I advised him that the radiologist needed to be accurate in his readings.

When the results were returned, I was now diagnosed with a hernia. I was grateful for the time that I invested in learning to read scans. Additionally, I made incredible contacts from around the world. I was given a referral to a surgeon and discharged from the facility.

The suffering and emotional turmoil that all of these radiologists caused me, and my family for 17 months was tremendous. Since January 19, 2019, I had complained about the deformities and discomfort in my abdomen along with my inability to take a dump, and it was ignored by these inept radiologists. This causes me alarm in knowing that this is the

KARRIE SICELY

best that we have to offer in our medical care system.

Why did I have to learn to read my own scans to find my hernia? Why did I have to locate an overseas radiologist to diagnose neurocysticercosis and confirm my hernia findings? There is no reason, that I can imagine, outside of protecting their own, every one of these professionals failed to diagnose my hernia.

In my soul a coverup was in place to protect Dr. Surgeon, and I was determined to find the proof. I decided to go out of state to Pittsburgh to a well-known facility to have my surgery performed. I called and made my appointment for July 8, 2020.

Major University

While driving my 9-hour trip, I called Dr. Overstreet to say hello and to discuss my surgery with him. The two of us spoke frequently, and I trusted his advice. Initially, I wasn't going to disclose to the surgeon that I had parasites and risk not getting treatment. Dr. Overstreet advised me against this, stating that it was important that the doctor be aware of my condition.

The anesthesia was a formidable consideration because it causes the parasites to migrate. If any of my cysts were penetrated it would cause me considerable harm from the parasites spreading. As usual, I would heed Dr. Overstreet's advice and do a full disclosure with my surgeon.

The following morning my father and I drove into downtown Pittsburg to see the surgeon. My dad agreed that he would accompany me to the exam room in case any gaslighting took place.

Once we arrived, we got checked in, waiting only minutes before being taken into the exam room. I was impressed with the speed of service that I received. We entered the exam room and the doctor arrived just minutes later. He stated that, after reviewing my scans, he found that I had two hernias, not one. I had both umbilical and epigastric. He further stated that, these were caused from my laparoscopic surgery. His honesty was amazing as I hadn't seen this level of ethics in a long time. His findings created more questions for me. How did the previous radiologists not see BOTH hernias? The story continues to get more disgusting as time goes on.

The surgeon said he could not fix the umbilical hernia but only the epigastric hernia. I went on to explain that initially, I wasn't going to however I elected to do a full disclosure. I informed him that I had parasites.

I told him that anesthesia would cause them to migrate, causing further problems and to my amazement, this doctor knew this! He said he wanted to get clearance from both infectious disease and gastrointestinal doctors prior to doing any surgery. Both appointments were scheduled for August 25, 2020.

Finally, I thought, I might get a positive parasite diagnosis in my file!

Radiologists

I headed back home thinking about my plan for this surgery after I received clearance. I thought about all that had happened and decided I would file complaints with both hospitals. On July 13, 2020, I called E-City hospital and spoke to the radiology director to file my complaint. I then called the hospital in Chesapeake and filed another complaint with their radiology director who said that he would call me back by Friday the 17th.

The director in E-City was apologetic and said that she was ordering peer reviews on all of my scans. She said that it would take some time and that she would let me know when they were completed. Later the director would advise me that I was not entitled to the results of the peer reviewed readings.

Friday the 17th came, and I received a call, but it wasn't from the hospital director of radiology. It was Dr. Radio, who was the director of the radiology firm, that did many CT scans on me. We spoke for 38 minutes covering many topics including parasites.

I was very concerned that several of their radiologists failed to diagnose my 2 hernias. He apologized while reviewing my scans on his computer screen as we spoke. I told him that the surgeon in Pittsburgh had diagnosed 2 hernias: the epigastric and umbilical, stating they were caused from my laparoscopic surgery.

He said, "yes I do see the hernias and I do see where they were caused from the surgery." He apologized that his team had let me down. What he didn't understand was that all the money, travel, emotional turmoil that my family had gone through was far more than just letting me down.

As we talked, I inquired about his knowledge of reading parasites in scans. I was shocked when he told me that he had not learned anything about that, further stating that it was not included in his educational program.

He continued to tell me that he was aware of parasites because he grew up on a farm. They had to be careful in all of their activities, so as not to contract parasites from the animals. I shared my journey with him up until that point in time, divulging that I had parasites and how western medicine had all but killed me.

As we were closing our conversation, I told Dr. Radio that I needed a new report with his comments in it. His response said it all! He said, "I can do new reports, but I can't put that in it" I asked why. He said, "I can't go against another doctor." I told him that he didn't need to be concerned with Dr. Surgeon, who I had thought they were protecting and that he was retiring effective the 30th.

He said, "no you don't understand, I can't go against another doctor." This comment stayed deep in my mind for the next 6 months, until I was awakened from a dream. I got the message loud and clear. Dr. Radio and the other radiologists were not protecting Dr. Surgeon. They were protecting the very first radiologist who did not diagnose my hernias in the scan performed on May 6, 2019! While I knew there was a cover-up, I had no idea that it was to protect one of their own.

Dr. Surgeon's sudden retirement was now making sense to me. I remembered that I left a voicemail on his nurse's phone in May 2020, asking for Dr. Surgeon to review my scans so that he could find the unfortunate problem that he caused. He probably did review my scans, only to discover that he caused me 5 hernias. If I am right, this was the biggest plan of conspiring against a patient that I had ever seen. I would have never thought that this could happen in this country, but it did. If this happened to me, I thought, how many others had this happened to?

The following Friday I went to the hospital in Chesapeake to pick up my new reports only to find that Dr. Radio failed to note TWO hernias. We had spoken about them, and he admitted that he saw them, so why were they not both noted? I still don't know to this day what the answer is. He has refused to take any further calls from me.

I continued to search for a lawyer to assist me in a lawsuit only learning that hernias caused by doctors or surgical equipment was considered "standard of care." This means that any doctor could cause extended injuries during the surgery, and it is not considered malpractice.

ID and GI in PA

I began my second trip to PA for my appointment on August 24, 2020, to see the infectious disease and GI doctors. I was interested to see what diagnosis they would give me, as well as what testing they had to offer, that was so much better than everyone else's. I already had Dr. Overstreet, who identified cysticercosis, and two other parasitologists who said the same thing.

This time I took my sister with me. We went into the office, doing the usual check-ins, and we were taken to the exam room. Dr. Gastro2 came in with two interns following behind him. Initially he seemed fine and didn't display any sign of aggression that I had seen previously with other doctors at the mention of parasites. I began to explain what had been going on, and that I had received treatment for parasites. I needed clearance for surgery to ensure that my parasites were all gone, making it safe to do my procedure.

Dr. Gastro2 didn't seem to be interested and started to behave as so many before him had. His manners and expressions were rude, proving to me, that he didn't believe that Americans could have parasites. As proof, I brought my empty antiparasitic medicine bottles with me and asked if he wanted to see them, but he was not interested. At this point, I thought that it was funny after seeing this happen with so many doctors prior to him. What was it that was causing the change in the demeanor of these doctors when anyone said the "P" word? I had already done so much research and had pieced together many pieces of this puzzle.

The GI doctor ended the conversation stating that he didn't see any reason that I couldn't have the surgery, abruptly ending this visit. I would later see that in my chart, on the app, that that Dr. Gastro2 made mention that he didn't believe that I had ever received treatment. I think that this was accidently put into the wrong file, allowing me to see it!

Our next appointment was with Dr. L at Infectious Disease. We checked in and was taken back to the exam room a brief time later and Dr. L entered the room. I began to explain once again that I had parasites which required clearance for surgery. She admitted that she didn't know much about parasites but wanted to order some labs. She had left the room a couple of times so that she could go research about parasitic infections and testing methods. She said that she would submit one test to the CDC.

The phlebotomist came in to draw blood. This was my opportunity to question her experience level. Her answer was indicative that she had little experience, however, I was willing to allow her do draw my blood. She blew a vein in both my left and right arms. The phlebotomist left the room to get the nurse who came in and looked at my arms. Because of the location of the draws they could not attempt to perform another one. I would have to return the following day to try again.

The following day my sister and I returned to the ID department to complete the blood draw, but this time I had the expert completing the task without incident and I headed back to North Carolina.

As it turned out, the doctor entered the wrong code for my lab order for CDC testing, so they instead sent my labs to LabCorp.

The results on my phone app showed that my results were negative, and the doctor cleared me for surgery.

I sent a message to the surgeon and told him that I was ready to have my epigastric hernia repaired. I was then informed, that I had to quit smoking for thirty days. A month later I sent another message that I had been free from smoking and was ready for my surgery. I called and sent messages on my app, yet they never responded. After a few attempts, I concluded that the notes Dr. Gastro2 put in my file caused Dr. Surgeon2 to change his mind about performing the surgery. What was it with all of these doctors putting bullshit lies in my files?

Move To Florida

We decided to move for medical reasons as well as to be near our new grandbaby. We bought a home when we went to see the new baby in June 2020. We packed up the U-Haul truck and planned to leave the following day, heading to our new home. I noticed that one of my German Shepherds wasn't acting right. Daisy is the dog that had heartworms and had received even more intense treatments than I had. I decided to monitor her for a little while to see if she just didn't feel well and if she would improve on her own.
It had been less than 24 hours since I noticed that she wasn't feeling well and was progressively getting worse. That is when I alerted the boys that we had to take her to the hospital. She was unable to walk, so the boys put a blanket under her and carried her to our car and we left.

Once we arrived at the vet's office, I checked her in and returned to the car where we waited for her to be seen. After an hour I complained that my dog had not yet been seen. My dog was dying! I explained again that this was an emergency, and I was told that Daisy was next on the list.

Our regular vet was not there, however an intern saw us. They finally took her back and performed a scan on Daisy. Her uterus had ruptured, and her blood was infected due to the toxicity from her ruptured uterus. The intern suggested that it was best to put her down. The three of us were devastated and began to cry. I had fought so hard for her survival against the parasites and putting her down was too difficult to accept.

143

I wasn't working at the time and had spent every penny of my retirement trying to find the help that I needed to   treat my parasite situation. I had nothing left. It wasn't fair for me to ask my husband to make yet another monetary concession after he had worked so hard for it. We spent about 20 minutes saying our farewells to Daisy when the intern returned. He stated that our vet had advised him that he would and could save her. The cost would be several thousand dollars, but for my soul it was worth it. I needed her to survive, so that I could. In my mind, I knew that if she survived, I would. I couldn't bear the thought of putting her to sleep after all we had been through. We had both fought parasites at the same time. How was I to deny her this help?

My husband looked up at the intern and said, "you couldn't have told us that before now?" in a jokingly manner and gave his approval for the vet clinic to proceed with the surgery. This delayed our move by a couple of weeks, but that was OK. Once she was out of the hospital, we went ahead and had Bella undergo the same surgery to avoid any future issues. Once our dogs were cleared post-surgery, we left for our new home in Florida.

We moved into our home and it was now time for me to find new doctors. I decided to go with a female doctor in hopes that she could better relate to all that I had been through. All of the doctors that I had seen up to this point were men.

My anxiety attacks and abdominal pain continued to bring me to tears. Was it the IBS that was causing this pain or was it my parasites? I didn't know, but I had to keep working to find the answers. I had to keep talking and teaching if I was going to make a difference in the lives of those who continued to suffer. But that wasn't my only goal, it was the future and health of my family that was my driving force.

The more vocal that I became related to parasitic infections in the United States, the more people I attracted to my social media sites. People started joining in, speaking publicly about their parasites. Increasingly, people spoke out publicly, giving a voice to all. My goal was to remove their shame that kept them in the shadows of private forums. There was and still is, a parasitic epidemic taking place in our country. People are pissed, they have every right to be and I, too am pissed. Many of those suffering had been diagnosed with delusional parasitosis, which is a bullshit diagnosis.

There was one person that I felt could make a difference and that was President Trump. I sent several emails through the White House contact link and never heard back. While I was disappointed, this would not deter me from exposing the truth! With or without them, we will tell our stories and force change.

It was early September when I had another anxiety attack. Being new to Florida, I needed to find the best hospital that I could. I asked my husband to take me to the ER. He didn't think that I needed to go but obliged me. We went to SJH for my abdominal pains and for the fact that, I just didn't feel good. I brought my scans with me, but once again, they wanted to do their own. This was the first radiologist who diagnosed me with 2 hernias in a report. Yes, I had a surgeon who had identified 2, but not a radiologist.

They did a urinalysis on me that showed a UTI, but they never gave me anything for it. I made my appointment with my new PCP to address my 2 hernias and treat my UTI. On my first appointment with Dr. W, she listened to me for an hour and a half crying, while trying to explain all that I had gone through. This was only the second time that any doctor other than Dr. Beard spent this much time with me. I held a lot of anger in my heart for everything the doctors had put me through up to this point and I didn't hide it well.

I could tell that she was unsure of what to make of me and that was OK. She at least listened to me and that was worth more than she knew. This would be the beginning my healing journey in my thoughts and heart. She made a comment about my visible anger towards all doctors, and I realized that she was right. It would be after this appointment when I reflected on what she said and realized that I my grudge towards ALL doctors was not fair. I worked hard to adjust my feelings.

When we reviewed the ER notes from my visit at SJH, she asked me if they gave me any medications for the UTI. She was surprised when I told her that they did not. She ran another urine test to identify which bacteria I had. The results came back showing that I had an elevated level of E. Coli in my urine. She prescribed medicine, which alleviated my symptoms only for a short spell. I have had several more UTIs since.

Now remember that I ordered my own lab back in December 2019 that showed I had high E- Coli and Klebsiella in my stools, but no one would treat me for them. The only one who did was the Urgent Care in 2020 when I resulted with another UTI.

I asked her for an order to have an ultrasound of my abdomen completed, thinking they might see more than what the CT scans had shown.

She gave me the referral and I went to the radiology firm who performed the scan. The results came back that I had 3 hernias, all with omental tissue in them as well as a swollen liver with cysts and lesions. They call this a fatty liver.

According to the CDC, hernias with omental tissue is very uncommon, but doctors think it is quite common and no big deal. The information provided on the CDC is contradictory. Who is right? Is this common or uncommon? Either the CDC or the doctors need to change their statements. If the CDC is right, then the doctors need to be re-educated. If the doctors are correct, then the CDC needs to correct their reports.

If you remember, Dr. PCP2 initially said that I had a swollen liver and spleen on December 4, 2019, then retracted his diagnosis after the university said they didn't see anything. Now I have this proof that they both were wrong.

My hospital records from 2019 (back when I was losing organs left and right) show that my liver was 17.76cm in size when the normal size for a woman was 7-8cm. They knew that I had a problem, and this could have killed me but never considered that my life meant something to my family or even me.

With so many unsettled medical issues, I tried to address them one by one. I needed to see an ear nose and throat (ENT) doctor regarding this lesion above my tonsil. This was the lesion that the nurse practioner removed, when she exclaimed that it looked like a worm. I also needed to see a GI and an orthopedic to address my abdominal pain and broken foot.

I scheduled an appointment with Dr. ENT as well as a new GI. My appointment for the GI was going to be before the ENT. I arrived at the new GI's office and began to explain what was going on. He wanted to do a colonoscopy which was scheduled for November 3, 2020.

We arrived at the surgery center. After my procedure, I was advised that the doctor removed a few more polyps. It was making even more sense now. Polyps were a sure indicator of a parasitic infection. Why do I say this? I say this because it is NOT normal for our bodies to just develop growths, not to mention that in my research, it was clearly stated that there were connections to parasitic cysts.

I know that many people may disagree with my opinions about parasites, and that is OK. Those who disagree may just need to do some research of their own, utilizing all of the available search engines. These are my opinions, and I will forever believe that they are correct. I am not a scientist, nor do I have to be, to add all of these pieces of this puzzle together. It would seem like common sense to me.

I asked this new GI if he could refer me to a surgeon for my hernia repairs, and he did. I only had one stipulation and that was to have a surgeon from another country that was familiar with parasites. I needed a surgeon that would know what he was looking at when he opened me up so that if he saw a parasite, he could remove it without getting freaked out. I was referred to Dr. Surgeon2.

There was no time to waste as my appointment with the ENT was approaching. I needed the lesion in my mouth to be examined, the inflammation in my tonsils to be addressed, and hopefully, the lump in my lip removed. I knew that it was a parasite because I could feel it move at night, but I wasn't about to tell the ENT.

On my first visit he did his examination and said that these lesions were known to cause cancer. He also stated that my tonsils may have to be removed because of the amount of tonsil stones and inflammation. I knew they were all related to the parasites, but I wouldn't say anything just yet. He went ahead and removed most of the lesion from my mouth. Parasites often lodge themselves into the tonsils. According to the University of Michigan, it is not just bacteria invading the tonsils because parasites do as well. Symptoms can appear to be tonsilitis and very well could be caused by bacteria however, the medical professionals are not checking to see if it is parasitic in nature.

His statement that lesions can turn in to cancer was interesting. I had read studies that show that parasites have cancer cells in their body naturally, causing many misdiagnoses that leave many individuals undiagnosed. The CDC released an article stating that cancer cells from parasites had been found in human tumors. This has since been archived and not available to the public.

I still had to get my broken foot examined by an orthopedic surgeon. I scheduled my visit and went to see Dr. L who is a young knowledgeable doctor. He did an x-ray in the office and confirmed that I did have a bone that appeared to have healed much higher than it's original location. He also saw where the pins from my bunionectomy had gone through the bone in my foot and said that he could fix both. My X-ray images and reports are available to view at my website, TheParasiteLady.com

We scheduled my surgery for February, but my physical didn't go so well. We had to postpone it to April 7, 2021. In Florida, doctors require a full physical prior to surgery. This never happened in Hampton Roads, I do not understand why this was not done in the past? After all my tests came back, I received clearance to proceed with my surgery.

At my 2-week follow-up, Dr. L informed me that the bone was free flowing. He said he opened it up and simply picked up the bone and removed it. Prior to my surgery, I told him that it felt like my bone was moving inside my foot. He removed the pins that had penetrated through my bone, allowing me to walk freely without catering to my foot. Dr. L is a blessing to me.

Remember the doctors at the orthopedics' offices in Norfolk and Virginia Beach? The orthopedic saw one fracture, were lost on the information about the pin, and the surgeon didn't see anything wrong? Was it when I mentioned that I had parasites that they became blind? The delayed treatment forced me to walk on a broken foot for 17 months. Once again, the doctors are not held accountable.

In the spring of 2020, prior to us deciding to move, I researched doctors who could help me that were educated regarding parasites. That is when I had found Dr. Axe, at the Root Cause Clinic known as Axe Holistic Care. I called him last year and we began to talk about parasites. He was well educated on human parasites. I couldn't get to Florida at that time, however since our move, I was able to pursue his care and expertise.

I had gone to see Dr. Axe and explained to him everything that I experienced along with the symptoms that I was still having. I wasn't sure if I still had parasites because I had already received numerous treatments. He ordered several labs to discover many deficiencies in my nutrients which I worked to correct.

I took herbal supplements each day that not only stopped my tears from flowing but stopped my IBS. Earlier in this book, I discussed that I needed to get to the root cause of my ailments and now was I getting help from the Root Cause Clinic.

In February of 2021, Dr. Axe also ordered labs for my phlegm and stool. The reports from testing showed substantial, elevated levels of bacteria. In the past I have resulted with E. Coli numerous times and continue to struggle with these bacteria in my lungs and my kidneys.

If you remember, I spoke briefly about what I called renal failure earlier in my book. I believe that this is caused by the elevated bacteria. This is often, not tested for, and is overlooked. Also, I had E. Coli and Klebsiella at elevated levels since December of 2019 and continued to battle UTI infections. I have learned just how difficult it is to get me levels to a normal range. I continue to work on these issues.

The proper treatment that Dr. Axe provided me has tremendously reduced my pain levels. The treatment did not diminish the feeling of a tight belt inside me that is caused by the hernias. I have yet to find a doctor to perform my surgery.

Without any effort, I also lost 50 lbs in just 8 months. I sleep soundly throughout the entire night and wake up feeling rested with a lot more energy. I still have difficulty eating a full meal therefore I continue to consume ridiculously small amounts of food more often. I still cannot lay on my stomach and struggle to lay on my sides. This is particularly difficult for me because I am not a back sleeper. If I eat past 4 PM I will not be able to go to sleep until 3 or 4 AM because of the pressure in my stomach. I am not as healthy as I was prior to getting parasites, however

I have very much improved. I can now think clearly, I don't cry, I can walk and there is little pain in my body other than my hernias.

I consulted with another surgeon who specializes in hernia repairs. My scans were sent directly to his office from the radiology firm. The doctor claims that he never received them, and the radiology firm claims that they were sent out. As a backup, I took my 30 or so scans with me, just in case he wanted to review them, but he wasn't interested. He performed a physical examination and told me that he didn't care what any hospital or doctor said, and that I did not have any hernias. Say what?? Talk about confusing! Now I don't know if I am coming or going once again.

How could I still not get two doctors to agree whether I had hernias? Could the parasitic cysts in my abdomen give the appearance of hernias? It is not wise to have someone cut on me until I find out if I have hernias or if I have parasitic cysts mimicking hernias. It would be insane to do this.

My new GI referred me to a surgeon who met my criteria. I checked-in and met with Dr. Surgeon. I had my scans with me, in case he wanted to review them, and he did. He stated that we had to get the epigastric hernia fixed for sure, but not until my bacteria levels were reduced. On the following visits he made it impossible for me to have the repairs completed because he wanted clearance that the cysts were gone. As I mentioned before, cysts can be viable for up to ten years. I have yet to find an American radiologist skilled in identifying parasites on scans. The only way that I can accomplish this is to have my doctor order an updated scan and for me to send it overseas.

I will continue to fight my way through the suffering until I find the proper medical professionals to perform my hernia repairs. Hopefully this will get me back to eating normally again. I do believe that when someone fixes my hernias, that the bacteria will stop leaking into my body, allowing me to fully recover.

My last passing of parasites was May 27, 2021, when I introduced a new product to my regimen. I ran out of microscope slides, not expecting to pass anymore parasites. I placed the specimens in a petri dish, and they are now in a freezer where they will remain until I need them for evidence.

I made one more trip to the ENT doctor to discuss cutting out the lump in my lip. I finally disclosed that I had parasites. Remember during my first visit with him, he stated that he could remove the lump, but he needed to perform the procedure in a hospital setting since lips bled a lot. After I disclosed that I had parasites, he was no longer willing to perform this procedure. So, I still have the worm in my lip until I find a doctor who is willing to remove it.

Conclusion

I t is important for me to break down and analyze all that has happened to me and why! I am simply using critical thinking skills to understand why millions of Americans and people around the world cannot get help for parasitic infections.

Back in 1997 I had a PCP who believed that I had MS. I had enormous amounts of pain in all my joints. As I would reach for a coffee cup and grasp the handle, the pain in my elbow was excruciating to the point that I could not lift the cup. The doctor found no lesions in the MRIs performed on my brain and spine. He said that it could take years before they appeared.

He continued to have MRIs done on my brain every 6 months until I got tired of doing them and stopped. Looking back, it makes me question, whether or not, this is when it all started with my deteriorating health condition. Looking at what we know today about MS, my body aches and a single pimple blister may have been the key indicators of a parasitic infection.

With my research, reading many medical studies, it became clear to me that cancer is parasitic. This makes sense to me; we are always asked about our family history of cancer because it is believed to be genetic. A pregnant woman can pass cancer on to her offspring. Can she also pass parasites on to them as well? The CDC article that disclosed that they found parasitic cells in human tumors was now adding up.

There are vast quantities of studies relating parasites to every human disease that we see today. When I examine the countries that are well versed in parasitology, the correlation became evident: that they also have extremely low cancer rates. These are the very countries that teach the science of parasites in their medical schools, their doctors treat their patients. Their communities at large, are well versed and educated regarding parasites as well.

I have researched and found that every medical issue that I have had is related to my parasites. So, we must start asking, why are we not told of the connections between parasites and our diseases?

How do we humans contract parasites and why do so many of us have them? Parasites are the earth's cleaners. They clean toxins and metals from our soils, allowing us to have healthy foods for consumption. Chemtrails are being sprayed through-out the world. We are exposed in multiple ways, causing us to become toxic with metals. Parasites as the worlds cleaners are naturally attracted to these metals and absorb them. This is how we are contracting these parasites and why so many have them. We have become toxic, making us the hunted. Although we are not the natural hosts for these parasites, we have become extremely appealing to them, thereby attracting them. We are now highly sought after as hosts. It is imperative that we detox our bodies to eliminate parasites, the enemies within.

My research took me back to the early 1900's where I discovered how we managed to get to this point. It is a lot of information and far too much to disclose in one book. Our grandparents were well versed in parasites and herbal medicine therapies of the day. My grandparents were born back in the 1900's and were well versed in natural remedies. The next generation, those born in the 40's were the first to use allopathic care. Medical practitioners are not being taught about parasites, so they are not able to help their patients. When the Rockefellers infiltrated the educational system to gain wealth from pharmaceuticals, the health of our world changed to our detriment. See, they wanted the ability to use their oil by-products in medicines and vitamins, which many of us take daily. And we don't know why we are all sick.

Let us analyze other means of contraction. We know that mothers can pass parasites on to their unborn children, a prime example is toxoplasmosis. But what about blood donations? The donated plasma is only tested for specific parasites being surveilled by the CDC. The following parasites are not being surveilled; Plasmodium spp, Trypanosoma cruzi, Toxocariasis, Babesia microtia, toxoplasma gondii, and Leishmania spp and Hookworms. Surveillance means parasites are being tracked in human infections. With parasitic infections being so invasive and harmful, why is the CDC not tracking all of them?

Vectors like mosquitoes can spread filariasis and malaria, both of which are parasitic. Snails can transmit liver flukes and fleas transmit tapeworms. Therefore, it is not just food, water, dirt, or pools that are the sole pathways to infections. Currently, there is no surveillance of any of these vectors on a nationwide level.

Another issue is organ donations. I am not aware of any testing that takes place on the donated organs to check for parasites by the experts of parasitology. I hold the same concerns for anyone receiving skin grafts, bone marrow, stem cells or cartilage donations.

Surveillance, testing of blood , organs, and all vectors are all crucially important to discuss. To rectify this situation, we must understand where we failed.

Most Americans and people from a few countries have no idea about parasites. It is never a thought in anyone's mind nor was it in mine. Only those who get to the root cause and discover what ails them, like I have, understand the devastation of having parasites. Although those who suffer are speaking out, it appears that the individuals with closed minds cannot hear. Is it because they fear the truth? Is it too much for them to comprehend? Or was there some evil plan devised long ago that is still in full play? The answer is yes, they are all true.

We are repeatedly told by professionals in every field, that parasitic infections do not happen in the United States. What I will tell you is that this is a lie! How do I say this, you ask? I say this because the evidence is freely available to anyone who digs into do their own research.

There is an incredible number of studies on the CDC site as well other sites displaying these studies. The CDC released an article in 2014, that stated that 1 in 3 Americans had undiagnosed parasites. That translates to approximately 130 million Americans as that time. But how could they know if people are "undiagnosed?" I believe they are tracking ICD codes to come to this conclusion. What that means is that 130 million Americans have sought medical help and their testing did NOT result in a positive, so they found NO help or treatment from traditional medicine. That article was archived in 2020. So now we must ask another question. Why, if the CDC is fully aware of the epidemic of parasitic infections, are they not doing anything to disclose or help the people?

The answer is disturbing if I am right. The morbidity related to parasitic infections is massive. I lost 4 organs, have 5 hernias; swollen liver with cysts and lesions; Staph Strep in my lungs, E. Coli in my urine; fatty liver and neurocysticercosis to name a few problems. Can you see the money being generated from all I have been through, and I am still going through? This is about money! If we look at the revenue generated from cancer treatments in 2018 it was 5.6 billion US dollars out of pocket. The 2030 projections indicate that it will increase to $245 billion. Since cancer is such a huge money maker, is this why it is not recognized as a parasitic infection? The cost effectiveness to treat parasitic infections would bankrupt the medical industry.

Now let us discuss the non-disclosure of incidental findings. Let me define the term "incidental finding" if you go to see a doctor for a specific condition and the doctor finds something entirely different, they do not need to disclose that to you. It was noted in my charts that I had a swollen liver, but it was never disclosed to me. When I finally was diagnosed with a swollen liver, I went to a study that was implemented by Dr. Theordore Nash from the NIH. After performing their scan, I was informed that I couldn't join their study because my liver wasn't stiff enough. Read that again! They are waiting for my liver to get to the point that my life will be in jeopardy before they will help me. Why? Is it that they desire a larger profit from my illness? I don't know, but it sure seems that way. Is this why the incidentals are not disclosed? It seems there are more questions than answers.

So, then we must question the ethics and oaths of those who created these laws or polices, as well as those following them. Isn't it our right to get full disclosures?

It is not just the Chemtrails causing our toxicities. The amalgam fillings of mercury in the mouths of many are super toxic according to the WHO. It is the single most toxic and dangerous substance to a human being. Yet the ADA rebutted this statement. Again, was this about money? It takes a holistic dentist to remove these fillings to ensure it is done safely.

I am not a parasitologist or a scientist. I am only an expert in having parasites and fighting for my life. I am an expert in the detrimental effects on the human body and the devastation of the family unit. I am an expert in researching to find the answers, all of which I cannot disclose at this time.

We must remove all biases and unethical provisions to get this conversation started if we are to remedy this epidemic.

Parasites are not uncommon, just uncommonly diagnosed!

Thank you all for allowing me to share my journey with you and thank you for taking the time to read about my perspectives on this subject.

The End

◆ ◆ ◆

Invitation

◆ ◆ ◆

I would like to invite you to visit my website at
ParasitesInsideMe.com for additional resources to
assist you in your journey to eradicate parasites.

ABOUT THE AUTHOR

Karrie Sicely

KARRIE SICELY SHARES HER PERSONAL JOURNEY, ASTONISHING DISCOVERIES, AND THE TRUE NATURE OF HER MULTIPLE ILLNESSES. HER DETERMINISM TO FIND HELP EXPOSED AN EVIL AND DISTURBING WORLD.

PRAISE FOR AUTHOR

My name is Derrick Earley from Suffolk Va. I came to know Karrie about 3yrs ago when she became my manager at Lennox. Karrie and I hit it off from day one and became great friends, still to this day. I noticed right off the bat that she is an extraordinarily strong headed woman. She means what she says and says what she means.

We talked about God and our life experience during downtime at work which was a regular occurrence. Karrie used to complain about her head and stomach hurting. She said she felt like something was eating her alive from the inside of her body. Not long after this, Karrie asked if I had a weak stomach as she wanted to show me something to get my opinion. I was like sure, so she proceeds to show me a specimen of her bowels. I was kind of freaked out at what I was seeing. I notice little white things that look like worms to me. So as Karrie tried to research and find a doctor that would help her and diagnose her condition, I continue to pray and asked God to help heal her. I tried to be the pillow of hope that she needed at that time, because I know God to be a healer and hers was coming. I began thinking about all the trials and tribulations she had already won in her life I knew that this too, was just a test. When God has a calling on your life, the devil will try to distract you by bringing all these things on you; but if we just focus our attention on the healer, and not the situation, then by his words we are healed.

I just want to tell you Karrie, God knew that you could handle this, and he can use you to be the mouthpiece concerning this issue that plaques many Americans today. Continue speaking and teaching people about this issue.

Sometimes when we get off God's course, he must redirect us back to his will not ours. Thank you for showing me what courage looks like.

I Love You, my Friend.

- DERRICK EARLEY

MEDICAL DISCLAIMER

◆ ◆ ◆

Parasites Inside Me author Karrie Sicely makes no promises, guarantees, representations and or warranties regarding medical diagnosis and or medical treatment, and is neither diagnosing, preventing, nor treating specific health challenges.

You are solely responsible for your own medical care. All opinions and statements in this book are mine. They are not that of my endorsements.

Karrie Sicely

◆ ◆ ◆

Made in United States
Orlando, FL
24 September 2024

51920751R00104